JOBS in
the SUN

JOBS in the SUN

Gap year and career-break opportunities

Charles Davey

KOGAN PAGE

London and Philadelphia

C002.5
0014 1482
9/06

Publisher's note

Every possible effort has been made to ensure that the information contained in this book is accurate at the time of going to press, and the publishers and author cannot accept responsibility for any errors or omissions, however caused. No responsibility for loss or damage occasioned to any person acting, or refraining from action, as a result of the material in this publication can be accepted by the editor, the publisher or the author.

First published in Great Britain and the United States in 2006 by Kogan Page Limited

120 Pentonville Road
London N1 9JN
United Kingdom
www.kogan-page.co.uk

525 South 4th Street, #241
Philadelphia PA 19147
USA

© Charles Davey, 2006

ISBN 0 7494 4460 6

British Library Cataloguing-in-Publication Data

A CIP record for this book is available from the British Library.

Library of Congress Cataloging-in-Publication Data

Davey, Charles.
    Jobs in the sun: gap year and career-break opportunities / Charles Davey.
        p. cm.
    ISBN 0–7494–4460–6
  1.   Employment in foreign countries.   I. Title.
HF5382.55.D38 2011
331.702--dc22

2006009949

Typeset by Saxon Graphics Ltd, Derby
Printed and bound in Great Britain by Bell & Bain, Glasgow

Contents

CAMP AMERICA

Camp America is one of the world's leading summer camp programmes offering its counsellors 40 years of experience placing people from Europe, Asia, Africa, Australia and New Zealand at US Summer camps. Camp America looks to recruit people with skills, experience and qualifications in a wide variety of activities ranging from tennis and archery to arts and crafts.

If you're looking for a memorable summer, we offer you free flights, accommodation and food along with the opportunity to earn up to $1200 pocket money in return for your skills and enthusiasm. The hours are long but the works enjoyable and you'll make life long friends and have the chance to explore the US after leaving camp.

Here's the view of one former participant "Thanks to Camp America I've had the most awesome summer ever. The kids were good, the camp was great and the friendships made were even better! I had the time of my life and I don't think I'll be the same again. Meeting and getting time to hang with people from around the world for 9 weeks is something I'll treasure the most."

Our application process is 100% on-line and our payments have been divided into three bite sized chunks to make it manageable for even the tightest of budgets. Early applicant is advised so visit www.campamerica.co.uk to request your brochure and start your application.

CAMP AMERICA, 37a Queens Gate, London SW7 5HR
Tel: 0207 581 7373   www.campamerica.co.uk

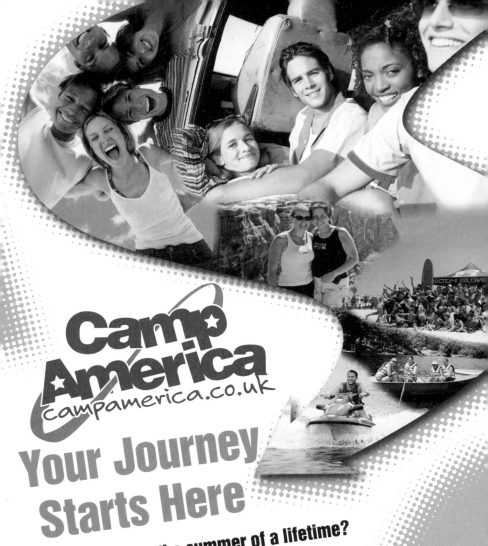

Preface

How many times have you woken up on a bitterly cold winter morning and wished you were living in the sun? It has become increasingly possible to realize this dream, and indeed thousands of people have done just that.

Within the last three or four years, existing airlines have substantially increased their range of services to the sun, and have been joined by several new players in the air passenger travel market. In the UK, easyJet has opened up new routes, as have Monarch, Ryanair and MyTravelLite, with GB Airways and Britannia recently announcing plans to significantly expand services from Manchester. Other new players include Globespan flying from Edinburgh and Glasgow, Jet 2 from Leeds/Bradford and Manchester, and Thomsonfly from Coventry and Doncaster/Sheffield.

This rapid expansion of passenger travel has been accompanied by, and indeed partially caused by, increased job mobility across Europe. Thanks to European regulations governing a wide range of occupations, EU member states must now recognize qualifications gained in other EU member states. Anyone from any member state now has the right to live and work throughout the EU, to have his or her professional qualifications recognized, and to pursue his or her occupation in Europe. A foreign EU national is to be treated by the authorities of any member state on exactly the same footing as its own nationals. This includes the provision of help and assistance in finding employment, setting up in business on your own account, and all other matters, including housing, social security and taxation.

Furthermore, many workers and businesses are benefiting from the services of EURES, which assists in job placements for those wishing to work in another EU member state, and provides practical help and advice, not just via its website, but also through its team of EURES specialist advisers placed across Europe.

In this book I have endeavoured to set out clear and concise guidance for those considering a move to the sun, both those intending to spend several months abroad, and those contemplating a more permanent move.

Acknowledgements

My thanks go to everyone at Kogan Page who has helped bring this book to publication.

1 The European Union (including general advice)

The European Union (EU) comprises Austria, Belgium, Cyprus, the Czech Republic, Denmark, Estonia, Finland, France, Germany, Greece, Hungary, Ireland, Italy, Latvia, Lithuania, Luxemburg, Malta, the Netherlands, Poland, Portugal, Slovakia, Slovenia, Spain, Sweden and the United Kingdom.

A citizen of the European Union is entitled to live and work anywhere within the European Union. There are generally no formalities required to search for employment, other than the possession of a valid passport. However, unemployment in most southern European countries is higher than in the United Kingdom, though in many there is a shortage of labour in certain sectors, notably in IT. As a foreigner you are already at some disadvantage in approaching local employers, even if you speak their language to a high level.

A teaching qualification, especially the Post Graduate Certificate in Education (PGCE) or a Teaching English as a Foreign Language (TEFL) qualification, will increase your chances of finding work, though earnings are generally quite low. If you wish to teach English, then your prospects of making a living are possibly the highest in Spain, where there are numerous English-language courses, attracting students from around the world.

General information

Unemployment benefit

If you are unemployed in the United Kingdom and have been registered as a job seeker for at least four weeks, you can arrange for Jobseeker's Allowance to be paid to you in an EU member state for up to 13 weeks. You must remain available for work until you leave, and the reason for your departure must be to search for work. You are required to register as seeking work with the local national authorities within seven days of your last claim for Jobseeker's Allowance in the United Kingdom. You should make enquiries at your local Jobcentre Plus office or Jobcentre to complete the appropriate forms. In particular, you should obtain leaflet JSAL 22. You should also be given an E303 and an E119 before leaving. The former is to allow you to claim benefit in the member state, and the latter establishes your entitlement to health care. If you are not successful in finding work during that 13-week period, then you will cease to be entitled to receive Jobseeker's Allowance unless you return to the United Kingdom. If you obtain a job in the United Kingdom, but then are unemployed again, you can receive a further 13 weeks of the allowance while searching for employment elsewhere in the European Union. Information on transferring your Jobseeker's Allowance is contained in leaflet JSAL 22 available from your local Department of Work and Pensions (DWP) office.

Payment of other UK benefits while living elsewhere in the European Union

The principle of free movement of labour within the European Union requires that citizens of member states should not be impeded from living and working in other member states. Accordingly, citizens of EU countries should not lose any of their rights to welfare benefits by moving to another member state. Those currently in receipt of invalidity and disability benefits, widows' benefits or benefits received as a result of an accident at work or an occupational disease, are entitled to have their benefits paid to them irrespective of where they choose to live. The relevant benefits should be paid gross and include any increases. Incapacity benefit will only be paid to those who have paid Class 1 or Class 2 and 4 National Insurance contributions.

Your existing entitlement to a UK state pension will be frozen, and you will receive a reduced pension from the UK authorities when you reach retirement age. For those approaching retirement, it may be worthwhile making voluntary payments to bring your National Insurance contributions up to the level entitling you to a full pension. You should contact the Pension Service's International Pension Centre (part of the DWP on tel: +44 (0)191 218 7777) and the Inland Revenue's Centre for Non-Residents (tel: +44 (0)845 070 0040). Ask for up-to-date information and advice, including whether you should pay Class 2 or Class 3 contributions. The former is the more expensive option but entitles you to incapacity benefit.

Attendance Allowance and Disability Living Allowance are not normally payable once you move abroad permanently, unless you first became entitled to the allowances before June 1992. If you are living in another member state but remain liable to pay UK income tax and National Insurance, you or your spouse are entitled to claim child benefit from the UK authorities. This is not means-tested.

Entitlement to state benefits in the host member state

For those who are not in receipt of benefits when they leave the United Kingdom, but subsequently meet the eligibility criteria, the rules are different. Generally, you are insured by the country in which you work and pay tax and social contributions. Those who work in more than one EU country are governed by the rules of the country in which they live. Contributions that you have paid in your home country (or any other member state) should be taken into account in determining your rights to benefits. Accordingly if you lose your job in the host member state, you are entitled to claim unemployment benefit from its authorities. They should take into account the National Insurance contributions you have paid in the United Kingdom or any other EU country. You should ask your Jobcentre Plus office or Jobcentre for the forms you would need to enable you to make a claim in another member state.

You should also consider obtaining the guide 'Social security for migrant workers' available from the DWP, Pensions and Overseas Benefits Directorate, Tyneview Park, Whitley Road, Benton, Newcastle-upon-Tyne NE98 1BA, tel: +44 (0)191 2187777. It is also available from www.europarl.eu.int/factsheets/ 4_8_4en.htim. In addition there is a practical guide produced by the EU, *Your Social Security Rights when moving within the EU*, available on the internet at www.europa.eu.int/comm/ employment_social/sec-prot/scheme/guide-en.htm.

EURES (European Employment Services)

The European Commission sees greater mobility of labour as a key factor in the economic growth of the EU and for promoting political integration within the European Union. It has set up a cooperation network to liaise with the national employment services of member states, to encourage free movement of workers. EURES seeks to ascertain where there are shortages of labour, and how these can be met. It also has the task of promoting the proper recognition of qualifications by the various member states.

Once you have decided to seek employment, or indeed to study, in another member state you should contact EURES. It is an invaluable source of information and advice about living and working in the European Union, and can assist you in obtaining employment. There is no charge for this service. Start by browsing the EURES website – www.europa.eu.int/jobs/eures – and considering the job offers listed at www.eures-jobs.com. The latter is regularly updated, and you can search by professions and regions. EURES is in the process of making all posts advertised by member states' public employment services accessible from this site. Those posts where the employer has expressed particular interest in taking on workers from other EU countries are marked with a blue flag. The EURES site also permits you to create a CV and make it available to employers and EURES advisers.

In addition to consulting the site, you should contact your local EURES adviser through your local Jobcentre Plus office. His or her job is to provide advice and assistance to jobseekers and employers, and he or she should put you in contact with the EURES adviser in the region in which you wish to work. Another useful source of information and assistance is the interactive programme *On the Move*. It is accessible via www.europa.eu.int. Go to the Ploteus Portal and then 'links'.

Help and assistance from the member state's advisory bodies

Workers from other members of the European Union are entitled to the same rights and benefits as nationals of the host state. This includes the right to school education, employment training courses, and access to public or subsidized housing. The host state may not impose unnecessary hurdles or conditions on access to employment or any rights or benefits in ways that indirectly discriminate against nationals of other member states.

Unsolicited letters of application

A surprising number of people obtain employment by sending unsolicited well-written letters and CVs to a wisely chosen selection of companies. You should find out as much as you can about a company before you write, and compose your letter with its likely requirements in mind. Always check the company's website for information about it, and to see whether it has a facility to accept an application by e-mail, and if it uses a standard application form. Even if you decide not to use the company's standard form, at least take on board the sort of questions contained on the form, which you are likely to be asked at some point. You can obtain a list of US companies operating in many countries in the US trade directory and international database for that country. They cost around £90 and are available from any US Chamber of Commerce or from www.americansabroad.com.

Your covering letter should be brief and to the point, hand-written and in perfect French, Italian, Spanish or other applicable language. It should include a summary of your qualifications and experience, state why you have chosen to seek employment with that particular company, and indicate the strongest points in your favour. Always use a white envelope, and attach the letter to your CV with a paperclip. Do not forget to include an international reply coupon if writing from outside the country to which you are applying, as well as a self-addressed envelope. It is important to appreciate that generally European business correspondence is more formal than in the United Kingdom, and you *must* follow a standard style. Your CV must be well structured, clear and concise. Compose each CV separately by adapting your standard CV to appeal to the particular employer. If you cannot fit your CV onto to two typed pages of A4 (without crowding the pages), it is almost certainly too long. Always use good-quality white paper, and include a translation if your CV is not written in the local language.

A useful starting point for the preparation of your CV is the EU's European Standard Curriculum Vitae. It is available in 13 languages and can be downloaded via the EURES website (www.europa.eu.int/jobs/eures). Photographs, certificates of qualification and references should not be sent with your CV, unless they have been requested.

Divide your CV into sections. You should start with personal details – full name, date of birth, address and contact details – then have a second section setting out brief details and dates of your educational and training history, with separate paragraphs for IT and foreign language training. The third section should cover your work experience. Always start with your most recent employment. Include the names of your present and former employers, dates employed and nature of job carried out. A fourth section can be included to deal with any information that you consider particularly pertinent to your application, such as a clean driving licence.

Job interviews

You should already have obtained some information about your potential employer before you made your application or submitted your unsolicited CV. Once you obtain an invitation to attend for interview, take the time and trouble to find out more. Ensure you are familiar with specialist vocabulary in the language that you would be expected to use if you were working for this employer. The vocabulary that you will be using on a daily basis will differ considerably according to the sector in which you are employed. Be extremely positive about the member state and its language. Do not run down your own country or your fellow nationals! You will need to have with you three or four copies of your CV in the local language, a translation of your degree and/or other qualifications, your passport and two passport photographs.

Employment in border areas

EURES also plays a key role in creating cross-border partnerships involving trade unions, employer organizations, regional authorities and vocational training services. In border areas, people often live in one country and work in another. They can obtain extremely helpful advice and assistance from EURES in relation to the administrative, legal or tax complications that they often encounter on a daily basis (see www.europa.eu.int/eures).

Getting your qualifications recognized

A wide range of occupations is subject to specific restrictions and regulations. You must make enquiries of the relevant professional body. In the past foreigners have found it difficult to get their qualifications recognized, and to establish themselves in other EU member states. In recent years, however, as officialdom has been obliged to adapt its rules to comply with European regulations, foreigners have found that the situation has improved considerably.

To obtain a high mobility of labour in Europe, it is imperative that employees can have their qualifications recognized Europe-wide. With this objective in mind the European Commission has set up a network of National Academic Recognition Information Centres (NARICs) throughout the European Union. They provide advice and information to educational institutions, students, teachers and businesses in relation to the academic recognition of qualifications and periods of study in other member states. NARICs, however, do not have the power to recognize foreign qualifications, as this is usually left to the individual institutes of higher education. You should note that it can take as long as 12 months or even longer to obtain official recognition, and therefore you should start the process as early as possible. It is worthwhile taking a look at the website www.enic-naric.net, where you will find further details and links to the NARIC websites of the United Kingdom and other member states.

The system of recognition of a qualification depends on whether the profession is regulated or not. Regulated professions are those to which access is restricted to those holding the required qualifications, such as law or medicine. Non-regulated professions are subject to a general system of recognition, based on the principle that a person fully qualified in one member state should have the freedom to exercise his or her occupation in all member states. Where there are differences between the training received in the United Kingdom and your host member state, the member state's authorities can require you to take an aptitude test, or a period of work experience. You should contact the government department responsible for your particular occupation. For additional information contact the member state's NARIC. It has overall responsibility for the validation and recognition of qualifications pursuant to the various European Directives. You will need to provide a certified copy of your academic and professional qualification (with an official translation), along with a certified copy of your passport. There is a modest fee payable.

The British Council (www.britcoun.org) also has information on education and equivalence of qualifications for different member states. In addition it is worthwhile taking a look at www.eurescv-search.com

The long-term objective of the European Union is for citizens to be able to treat both their qualifications and non-formal workplace learning as a 'common currency' which can be earned in one or more member states, but 'spent' in others. The European Credit Transfer System was introduced with this aim in mind, but more recently education ministers have announced plans to establish a European Higher Education Area by 2010 in which degrees would be more easily comparable.

In order to achieve improved transparency and recognition of vocational qualifications, a network of National Reference Points is being established in member states in order for comparisons to be made between different national vocational qualifications. The European Union also places a great emphasis on the concept of *lifelong* learning, and has developed a number of programmes to establish this aim, such as the Socrates programmes.

Those who are self-employed and want to have their *experience* recognized should contact the Department of Trade and Industry and ask for a guidance pack about having experience recognized (Certificate of Experience Unit, DTI European Policy Directorate, Bay 211/212 Kingsgate House, 66–74 Victoria Street, London SW1E 6SW tel: +44 (0)207 215 4648).

Difficulties in exercising your rights as a European citizen

Some member states, such as France, are rather slow to implement European directives. Accordingly, you may well encounter problems in exercising your rights as an EU citizen, especially in relation to the recognition of qualifications. Fortunately the European Commission has produced a guide, *Dialogue with Citizens*, to help those who encounter problems in exercising their rights to live, work, travel and study within the European Union. It sets out how to challenge adverse decisions, and explains how to obtain a remedy where the host state has not played by the correct rules. To access *Dialogue with Citizens* go to www.europa.eu.int, then to Ploteus Portal and then 'links'. In addition the EU has created SOLVIT, an official body to deal with failures of member states to implement European directives, with offices in all member states. If you are British you should contact the UK office, not that in your host member state. The UK contact number is tel: +44 (0)20 7215 2800; for further contact details see the website www.europa.eu.int/solvit/site/centres/index_en.htm.

Finding employment

A great many English speakers find employment within the Anglophone communities, especially in the more popular areas in France and Spain, particularly in the tourist industry, the yachting industry, security services, childcare and as domestic staff. A large number of expatriates find such employment without speaking or learning the language of their host state. However, if you wish to have any realistic prospects of obtaining employment with the majority of employers, you need to have a reasonable knowledge of the local language and a willingness to improve your level. You will find below the main resources available to assist you in your search for work.

Networking

In areas with large numbers of Britons, your chances of finding employment can be significantly higher if you take the time to join in the local expatriate scene, especially if you are not gifted at speaking the local language. You may well hear of vacancies 'on the grapevine'. Networking is also invaluable if you decide to set up your own business. Read the local Anglophone newspapers and magazines and consult their websites, and the sites of US and British Chambers of Commerce, on some of which you can place an advertisement setting out your qualifications and experience. Other options include placing notices on the notice boards of expatriate organizations, clubs and associations, shops, bars and even churches frequented by other English speakers.

Different job categories

Teaching

There are occasional job vacancies for qualified (and unqualified) teaching staff across a range of academic subjects in British, American and international schools throughout the world. An ability to speak the local language is not always a requirement. Often these posts are advertised on the website of the *Times Educational Supplement*, and also on the website of the European Council of International Schools (www.ecis.org). It is well worth also checking individual school websites from time to time. Other websites worth exploring are www.education.guardian.co.uk, www.tefl.com, www.tesjobs.co.uk, www.developingteachers.com and www.eslemployment.com.

Teaching English

There are a large number of language schools across Europe, with the highest concentrations in capital cities, and most notably in Spain. Do not assume that it will be easy to obtain a post. In France, for example, there is a strong preference for fellow French nationals, even when it comes to teaching English. The French believe that the British have little knowledge of the French education system and are ill-equipped to help pupils pass their examinations.

Each year a large number of British graduates and under-graduate students work in Europe as language assistants, speaking English to the students, giving information about English-speaking countries and assisting the English language teachers. Assistants, who are generally under 30, normally work about 12 hours a week and receive a modest but reasonable level of remuneration. Positions are available in some primary schools as well as secondary-level institutions. Further information is available from Assistants Department, Central Bureau for Educational Visits and Exchanges, tel: 020 7486 5101. Most applicants apply from the United Kingdom.

Interpreters and translators

As trade between the United Kingdom and other EU member states continues to grow, and more and more British live and work in other parts of the European Union, there is an increasing need for interpreters and translators. Nevertheless there is considerable competition, and professional translators work hard to establish and keep a client base. The best-paid work is technical and legal translation, though this is often the most difficult, and can be rather dry. You can obtain information about working with languages from the Institute of Linguists (www.iol.org.uk). See also www.languagejobs.org. Within European Community institutions there is a considerable demand for translators and interpreters with high levels of skills. Details of posts can be found on the website of the European Communities Personnel Selection Office (EPSO): www.europa.eu.int/epso.

Information technology

If you speak another EU language fluently, and have qualifications and experience in IT, you should find no difficulties in obtaining employment in the relevant member state. This is a sector in which there is a shortage of experienced personnel. Considerable numbers of EU nationals working in IT, in particular from France, have moved to London to improve their skills, though many stay longer than they intended because of the considerably higher salary levels in the United Kingdom.

Secretarial and office work

Those with word processing experience and a high level of skill in an EU language are well positioned to find secretarial work, especially in capital cities, and along the Spanish Mediterranean coast. Even if you are seeking work within the expatriate community, a good level of the local language will be required. A working knowledge of Italian is a substantial advantage on the Côte d'Azur, as is a good level of German on Spain's Mediterranean coastline.

The yachting industry: recruitment and training

There is a high demand for yachting crew and personnel in the areas bordering on the Mediterranean, notably along the coastlines of southern France, eastern Spain and Italy. A useful publication with information and contact details for all three countries is *Yachting Pages* (www.yachting-pages.com). The main agencies for recruitment and training in the yachting industry include YPI Crew (+33 (0)4 92 90 4610); Camper & Nicholson (www.cnconnect.com); Global Crew Network (+44 (0)870 9101 888; www.globalcrewnetwork.com); Fred Dovaston (www.yachtjob.com); www.yachtingpages.com; and Viking Recruitment (+44 (0)1304 240881; www.vikingrecruitment.com). Another very useful starting point is the Riviera Radio website (www.rivieraradio.mc).

Domestic staff

Agencies include: Greycoat International (tel: +44 (0)207 233 9950, e-mail: info@greycoatplacements.co.uk; website: www.greycoatplacements.co.uk), and Fleurs de Provence (www.fleursdeprovence.com, tel: +33 (0)4 93 34 60 73). The latter has a regular demand for housekeepers, personnel to carry out household repairs, catering staff, gardeners, nannies and cleaners. Another agency, again in the south of France, is Oasis Services, tel: +33 (0)4 93 65 61 23.

Nursing

See www.graduatenurse.com. There has been a substantial shortage of nurses in France, and the authorities have recently carried out a campaign to recruit nurses from Spain, where salaries are lower. There is a high demand for medical, nursing and health service staff in all tourist areas during the summer, when demand is at its highest and permanent staff are on holiday.

Job placements

Those who have only recently joined the job market may succeed in obtaining a traineeship or job placement in another EU country with one of the larger multi-national employers (such as Unilever – www.you-unilever.com). This is an ideal opportunity to improve a foreign language, experience life in another EU country and assess whether you might wish to make your future there. If you are a student you might benefit from one of the work experience programmes. Details of many of these can be obtained from the International Association for the Exchange of Students for Technical Experience (IAESTE), Educational and Training Group, British Council, 10 Spring Gardens, London SW1 2BN (tel: +44 (0) 207 389 4774, e-mail iaeste@britishcouncil.org, website www.iaeste.org.uk). In addition the European Union has schemes such as Europass and the Leonardo da Vinci programme which enable young people to carry out vocational training in other member states. A useful starting point is the British Council's 'Windows of the World' site at www.wofw.org.uk.

Summer and seasonal work

There is a wide range of summer jobs available in southern Europe. These include jobs as sports instructors (especially water sports), crew and service staff for yachts, courier work, hotel and restaurant staff, gardening, representatives for tour operators, bar work, shop assistants, and fruit and grape picking. For many posts an ability to speak foreign languages is an advantage, and for others a clean driving licence or a qualification in first aid can be important. There is a major shortage of labour in some areas during the summer months, most notably on the Côte d'Azur, with around 300,000 temporary staff being recruited from mid-June to mid-September to cater for the millions of tourists who visit the region. Earnings in the hotel and holiday industries remain low, and in areas such as the south of France accommodation is expensive and often difficult to find. General websites that are worthwhile taking a look at are www.overseasjob.com, www.eurosummerjobs.com, www.summerjobs.com and www.resortjobs.com. A particularly useful book is *Summer Jobs Abroad* by David Woodworth and Victoria Pybus (2005).

Au pairs

In exchange for board and lodging with a family, and a modest allowance, au pairs look after children and also undertake varying degrees of housework. Some au pairs are treated very well, though many are expected to work very long hours and in some cases they are subjected to rudeness and cruelty. The agencies that place au pairs often state that they have carried out checks on the families offering to take au pairs, and this can provide some protection, albeit somewhat limited. Agencies often arrange local language classes and other activities, which can reduce the feeling of isolation reported by many au pairs.

Ideally try to meet the family before you commit yourself. Your employer is responsible for informing the member state's social security authorities that he or she has taken you on, and for making social security contributions on your behalf, which entitle you to health care under the member state's health system.

For those who are poorly treated, the best advice is simply to leave, even if you have signed a contract for several months. The chances of an employer taking legal action against you are very slight, and in any case if you have been treated badly you will not only have a good defence, you might have a claim against your employer. The best course of action is probably to ask the agency to find another post for you. Au pairs are often in short supply so it should be able to do this. Ensure that you always have sufficient money, or access to money, to return home. If you are without funds, consider asking your parents or a friend to pay your airfare. Failing this, seek assistance from the nearest British consulate, which could be prepared to lend you the airfare (see Appendix 1 for the addresses of consulates).

Voluntary work

There are numerous possibilities for voluntary work, although you normally need to be over 16 (or sometimes 18) and generally under 30. The work, which is often on archaeological or conservation projects, can be physically demanding. Though it is unpaid, board and lodging are provided. This is normally very basic and often subject to a modest contribution by you. Participants remain responsible for their own travel costs, insurance and health cover. You should note that the common language is frequently English, and you need to be careful in your selection if you are hoping to be immersed in the language of the member state.

General websites in English

www.europa.eu.int/jobs/eures
www.webseurope.com
www.exposure-eu.com
www.eurojobs.com
www.overseasjobs.com
www.escapeartist.com
www.justlanded.com

The contract of employment

While member states have different laws governing the relationship between employers and employees, and different tax rules and incentive schemes for employers, there has been increasing harmonization, especially over the last decade or so.

A contract of employment is an agreement between an employer and employee under which the employee agrees to carry out certain tasks in return for a wage or salary. It can be oral or in writing, but it is preferable to have a written contract, and most large companies do this. This document should record the names of the parties, the start date, duration (if temporary), the place where the employee will work or be based, the employee's professional category or a job description, and the basic wage or salary and additional benefits. It should also state the number of ordinary work hours required per week and the times at which the employee will be required to work, holiday entitlement, and the period of notice required. Lastly the agreement should identify any collective agreement between the employer and its workforce.

In addition to a basic salary employers often provide fringe benefits related to length of service, or bonuses including profit-sharing, distance and transport bonuses, workplace bonuses for difficulty of work, for unsocial hours, for dangers involved, or for quality or quantity of production.

End of the contract of employment

Contracts of employment can end by mutual agreement, retirement or resignation according to the contract terms; because they were for a fixed period of time that has elapsed; or through death or serious invalidity. They can also end as a result of natural disasters, redundancy, dismissal or constructive dismissal (where an employee justifiably leaves the employment in response to unacceptable conduct on the part of the employer).

Redundancy

If an employer wishes to make an employee redundant on economic grounds or because of a material change in the business, the host country should have laws setting out the procedure to be followed. The employer should make reasonable provisions for employees to undergo training and to adapt to the situation. It should investigate the possibilities of re-employment in the same or an equivalent job category, or if the employee agrees, consider a transfer to a lower employment category. In cases of large-scale redundancies the employer often has to put the case for a redundancy to the authorities by presenting a restructuring plan explaining why the proposed redundancies are necessary. The employer must allow employee representatives the opportunity of responding to the proposals. In France, for example, the employees can only be dismissed if the plan is approved.

Dismissal

An employer is entitled to discipline employees for misconduct, including physical or verbal abuse, fighting, theft, disobedience, drunkenness and breach of confidence. Employees are also at risk of dismissal when they refuse to accept a substantial change to an employment contract. Disciplinary action can include written and verbal warnings, and dismissal in the case of continued breaches, or a single breach if it is sufficiently serious. An employer is not permitted to dismiss an employee because of his or her ethnic origin, religion, sex or sexual orientation, political opinions, membership of a trade union, pregnancy, or for exercising a right, such as making a complaint. An employer may only dismiss on health or disability grounds if the correct procedures are adopted, including the obtaining of an appropriate medical opinion.

'Forced' resignations, and resignations 'in the heat of the moment'

If an employee resigns in response to unreasonable conduct on the part of the employer, he or she should state this in the letter notifying the employer of the decision to resign. In such circumstances, leaving can amount to 'constructive dismissal', which gives the employee the right to bring a claim before a tribunal for unfair dismissal.

You would be wise to take immediate legal advice before deciding to resign. If you resign on the spur of the moment, whether orally or in writing, in anger, despair or irritation, then your employer might be legally bound to accept your retraction if you change your mind. If you do wish to retract a resignation, do so as soon as possible, and in writing.

Restrictions imposed on employees

Employees must not use information that they obtain during their employment, such as trade secrets and lists of clients, for personal gain, and owe a duty of confidentiality to their employer.

Employers often try to extend this protection by including clauses in the contract of employment that seek to forbid or restrict the employee from working for competing companies after he or she has left the employment. If you are considering branching out on your own or moving to another employer, and suspect that you may be in breach of such a clause, you should take legal advice as to its enforceability.

Protection against sexual harassment

If you believe that you have been subject to harassment on the grounds of your sex you have a right to bring a complaint. Sexual harassment consists of the kind of behaviour that is aimed at obtaining sexual favours for the perpetrator or for another person. All employees are protected, as are job candidates and those on training courses. An employer must not penalize any employee who has suffered or refused to put up with sexual harassment, or who witnesses or reports such conduct. Any employee who considers that he or she has been prejudiced in any way, for example by a failure to be promoted, can bring a claim before an employment tribunal. Employees found guilty of sexual harassment should be subject to disciplinary action. Such conduct is often also a criminal offence.

Discrimination

European law prohibits sexual and racial discrimination, and also discrimination on the grounds of marital status, religious and political beliefs, trade union membership and disability.

Starting and running a business in Europe

Setting up a new business is fraught with difficulties even in your home country. Most new businesses fail in the first 12 months as a result of a variety of problems associated with inexperience, lack of planning, changing market conditions and plain bad luck. A major problem is lack of liquidity or cash flow, caused by overly optimistic sales forecasts and underestimating start-up costs. In most southern European countries the rate of new business creations is significantly lower than in the United Kingdom. Factors often include the heavy burden paid by businesses in social security payments, and the considerable bureaucracy faced by new businesses.

Those intending to start a business in a country not their own face added difficulties arising from the fact that they are operating wholly or partly in a foreign language, and in a system with which they may be unfamiliar. Inevitably these factors significantly increase the amount of time that they have to put into the business, as well as some of the start-up and running costs, which are only partly reduced if the business caters primarily for other English speakers. Whichever type of business you intend to run, you must be able to speak the local language to a reasonable level, or select a business adviser who is fluent in both that language and English, as well as experienced in advising businesses in the host country.

Obtaining advice and assistance

Good starting points for advice and assistance in English are the UK embassy of the host country, which is likely to have a number of leaflets and booklets available in English, any UK branch of that country's chamber of commerce, and the British and American Chambers of Commerce in the host country They often hold seminars, conferences, discussions and workshops. They are not only invaluable sources of information, but also useful means of establishing contacts with fellow English speakers running businesses in the host country, who have already overcome many of the difficulties that face newcomers.

There are a variety of state and quasi-state organizations that provide advice and assistance to those contemplating setting up a business. Other EU citizens are entitled to the same level of help and assistance as a citizen of the host member state. In most countries' unemployment offices you will be able to obtain help to find training courses, and advice on setting up your own business. In some centres you will be able to access various reference books and company listings. Some of the public employment agencies work hand in hand with partner organizations that offer job seekers the same type of service without charge. These often offer specialized assistance to particular groups such as the disabled, students and those working in specific sectors of the employment market.

Bank finance

A business plan is essential if you are to obtain a bank loan to finance your business. Indeed, this is something that you should carry out to protect the investment of your own input of capital and time. You will need to provide an assessment of the demand for your product or service, the competition, the likely revenue, the assets being introduced into the business, your fixed and variable costs and some cash flow forecasts. It is also vital that you adopt a marketing strategy. Many successful businesses spend up to half their income on marketing in the first months of trading, as they appreciate the importance of building a high market profile from the outset. Your plan must be based on reasonable assumptions. Avoid being over-optimistic.

Ideally your business plan should be organized in a loose-leaf binder that will enable you to easily revise parts of the plan when required. It should start with a brief summary of two pages at the most. This should be followed by a table of contents and sections dealing with the different issues in more detail, and finally the appendices where you can include copies of important documents or sources to which you have referred in the text.

Paying tax

Your tax liability is determined by your country of residence. The position becomes complicated when you change residency during a tax year. If, for example, you return to the United

Kingdom during the course of a tax year, you will become liable to pay UK income tax. You receive credit for tax paid to another EU state, but if you have paid no tax in that EU state, then you will be liable for the UK tax in full. Many people who have worked in two or more countries might in fact pay too much tax. The Inland Revenue can arrange for you to obtain a tax refund from the tax authorities of the other member state, though this can involve some delay. Otherwise you can deal with the authorities of the member state yourself, or alternatively you can use the services of a company such as UK Taxback, 1st Floor, 277–281 Oxford Street, London W1C 2DL (www.uktaxback.com).

2 Spain

Although unemployment in Spain is high, there are many Britons working in the country, notably in the popular coastal areas where most of the British residents have chosen to settle. Those with expertise in IT, or teachers of English, generally have little difficulty in finding a position in most Spanish cities.

Those coming from outside the European Union will need to provide the local Spanish consulate with a police certificate confirming that they have no police record, together with a translation. Once the document has been approved, they can make an application for a combined residence and work permit. They must satisfy the *Ministerio de Trabajo* that they have a work contract, and that no competent Spaniard or other EU citizen could be found to carry out the work. These applications are frequently handled by employers on behalf of their employees. A substantial number of foreigners obtain the assistance of a *gestor* (see below). Non-EU nationals who wish to start a business in Spain will need to prove that they have about US $140,000 to invest in Spain and that they will provide employment for Spanish nationals, or nationals of other EU member states.

The Spanish labour market

Despite having the highest level of economic growth in western Europe, Spain has the highest official level of unemployment. Unemployment rates are highest in Andalucia. While official unemployment is high, Spain also has the largest black economy in western Europe after Italy. The most industrialized regions are

Rioja and Navarra, whereas Galicia and Extremadura are known for their agricultural production.

The last decade has seen substantial immigration into Spain, mostly economic migrants who come primarily from Portugal, Ecuador, North Africa and Eastern Europe. In 2003 the annual number of immigrants reached 600,000, equivalent to 14 per 1,000 of Spain's population, the highest in Europe. Accordingly those in search of employment face fierce competition, especially for unskilled or semi-skilled work. Ideally you should find employment before you move to Spain. If you arrive without a job, do not assume that it will be easy to find one.

One sector where English speakers do have an advantage is in the teaching of English as a foreign or second language, a sector that employs several thousand native English speakers. Obviously if you have a teaching qualification, especially a Post Graduate Certificate in Education (PGCE), or a Teaching English as a Foreign Language (TEFL) qualification, your prospects of finding work are quite good, though generally the rates of remuneration are not high. Other sectors in which jobs are most in demand are tourism (though many of these posts are seasonal only), IT, financial services, sales, marketing and construction. On Spain's Mediterranean coast there are many jobs in the service industry, including beauty consultants, hairdressers, restaurant and pub staff, shop assistants, estate agents' representatives, satellite engineers and air conditioning engineers.

As to salaries, there is a considerable variation, with posts in Madrid and Barcelona generally commanding much higher salaries than elsewhere. Those employed in middle management or the professions can expect to earn within a range of €40–70,000. Average annual earnings for manual workers are in the region of €20,000.

Finding employment

There are numerous English speakers employed within the British community, particularly on the Costa del Sol and Costa

Blanca. Often they speak hardly any Spanish, even after years of living in the country. On the Costa del Sol, substantial numbers of expatriates work in the tourist industry, the yachting industry, security services, childcare and as domestic staff. Throughout Spain, there are a significant numbers of English speakers who teach English as a foreign language and have a TEFL qualification, and teachers with PGCEs working at one of the many UK or other international schools. However, while your chances of obtaining work will be increased by networking among other expatriates, or having a teaching qualification, if you are to obtain employment with a Spanish employer, a reasonable knowledge of Spanish and a willingness to improve it are essential.

EURES and *Oficinas de Empleo*

In Spain EURES advisers can be contacted via the local *Oficina de Empleo*. EU job seekers should register in person with their local office of the INEM or Instituto Nacional de Empleo or with the regional employment service. This is the most common means of obtaining information about job vacancies in Spain.

For more information see www.inem.es (mostly in Spanish only, although parts are also in English). There is a *Guide to Working in Spain* that you can download. General help and guidance is also available, including in English, at www.mtas.es. If you have applied to have state benefits transferred to Spain from your home country, you must register with your local employment office in Spain within seven days of leaving your home country.

Empresas de trabajo tempora (temporary employment agencies)

You can also make contact with recruitment agencies by sending them a CV and covering letter requesting an appointment. These agencies are only permitted to offer temporary work. They are listed under 'trabajo tempora' in the Yellow Pages (*Paginas Amarillas*). Some of the major public libraries in your home country may stock these, but the information is also accessible via www.paginasamarillas.com. It may also be worth contacting Manpower in your home country before leaving (its UK telephone number is +44 (0)207 224 66 88), Adecco (www.adecco.com) and Flexiplan (www.flexiplan.es).

The media

Scan the classified ads under *Ofertas de trabajo* (job offers) in the main newspapers, such as *El Mundo* (www.elmundo.es), *El Pais* (www.elpais.es), *El Periodico* (www. elperiodico.es), *La Razon* (www. larazon.es) and *ABC* (www.abc.es), and also the specialist weekly newspaper *Mercado de Trabajo*. The Sunday papers contain the largest recruitment sections. Salaries are seldom indicated in advertisements. Positions for management, professional and technical staff often appear in the *International Herald Tribune.* There are many English-language newspapers and magazines in Spain in which you will also find advertisements for job vacancies.

As well as the websites of the major Spanish newspapers, there is also an umbrella website for national and local press at www.mir.es/oris/enlaces/prensa.htm. Details of local English language publications are set out below. A number of radio stations, including some that broadcast in English, have job spots. On TV2 there is a regular jobs spot (at 9.30 am Monday to Friday) known as *Aqui hay trabajo.*

Network!

A huge proportion of jobs, both in the more popular coastal areas on the eastern side of Spain and in Madrid and Barcelona, are filled via personal contacts, especially for people who speak no or little Spanish. Networking is vitally important, both for finding out about vacancies and to ensure the success of any business enterprise. Make full use of the various foreign chambers of commerce (for the contact details of the American and British Chambers of Commerce see Appendix 1). Consult the various English-speaking newspapers and websites, and consider placing cards on the notice boards of expatriate organizations, clubs and associations, shops, bars and even churches frequented by other English speakers.

Employment guidebook

Each May a guidebook is published of the companies that offer employment in Spain. It includes a CD ROM that assists in searching for jobs, and is priced at about €16. Further information can be obtained from rmendez@fue.es. Another source for lists of potential employers is Kompass Spain. This includes a list of companies and can be consulted in main libraries and the Spanish Chamber of Commerce in your home country. See also www.kompass.es.

Unsolicited letters of application

Advice on this subject is contained in Chapter 1 on the European Union. Always look at individual companies' websites before applying. Look for a link *'trabaja con nosotros'* (work for us), or *empleo* (recruitment). Even if you decide not to use the company's standard form, at least take on board the sort of questions contained on the form, which you are likely to be asked at some point. In Spain business correspondence is more formal than in the English-speaking world. Open your letter with stock formal phrases such as *Muy Senor Mio* or *Estimado/a Sr/Sra*. The ending should be likewise formal, such as *'En espera de sus noticias. Le saluda atentamente'* followed by your signature (with your name typed underneath). Always include an international reply coupon if writing from outside Spain, as well as a self-addressed envelope.

Job interviews

Take the time and trouble to prepare yourself. Find out as much as you can about your potential employer. Be prepared to have your knowledge of Spanish tested, and also to be asked questions about your ability to settle in Spain, as well as why you consider yourself to be the ideal candidate for the post. Take with you three or four copies of your CV in Spanish, a translation of your degree and/or other qualifications, your passport and two passport photographs.

Qualifications

The NARIC (see page 8) contact details and address relating to Spain are:

> Maria Isabel Barrios
> Nieve Trelles
> NARIC Espana
> Subdireccion General de Titulos, Convalidaciones y
> Homoglaciones
> Paeso del Prado, 28
> E-28014 Madrid
> Tel: +34 (0)91 506 5593
> Fax: +34 (0)91 506 5706
> E-mail: misabel.barrios@educ.mec.es
> nieves.trelles@educ.mec.es

In Spain the regulated professions (in which employment is restricted to those holding the required qualifications) include architecture, medicine, nursing, midwifery, dentistry, veterinary surgery and pharmacy. A full list is available from the Ministry of Education, Culture and Sport (www.mec.es).

Further information is available from the *Subdireccion General de Titulos, Convalidaciones y Homoglaciones* at the Ministry of Education, Culture and Sport (see above for address), which is responsible for the validation and recognition of qualifications in Spain pursuant to the various European Directives. You will need a certified copy of your academic and professional qualification (with an official translation), and a certified copy of your passport. There is a fee payable of between €40 and €200 depending on the qualification. The process can take over 12 months.

Architects, doctors, lawyers, midwives, nurses, pharmacists and veterinary surgeons

All these professions are regulated by individual specific EU Directives, though these are soon to be replaced by a single Directive governing all regulated professions. You can access the Directives via the NARIC website (see page 8). All these professionals will, of course, also be subject to the rules and regulations of the relevant professional body in Spain.

Specific job categories

Teaching and teaching English

There are a considerable number of British, American and international schools in Spain offering a range of different subjects, and which periodically recruit staff. Posts are frequently advertised on the website of the *Times Educational Supplement*, and also on the websites of the European Council of International Schools (tel: +44 (0)730 268244; www.ecis.org) and the National Association of British Schools in Spain (www.nabbs.org).

There are a substantial number of language schools offering tuition in English, with many foreigners preferring to learn English in the warmth of Spain. The demand is such that most qualified teachers, including those with a TEFL or Teaching English as a Second Language (TESL) certificate should not have too many problems obtaining employment. Indeed, there are a good number of English mother tongue speakers teaching English without qualifications. Some of the schools prefer their teachers to have attended their own training courses. There are a considerable number of websites providing lists of employment positions, and plenty of opportunities to supplement the quite modest salaries with extra income. You will find language schools under *Idiomas* or *Escuelas de idiomas* in the Yellow Pages.

The British Council has regular vacancies for qualified language teachers with experience, and for supervisors in its language centres in Madrid, Barcelona, Bilbao, Palma (Mallorca) and Valencia (tel: +44 (0)20 7389 4167, www.britishcouncil.org). The British Council also keeps a list of language schools throughout Spain.

You will find advertisements of vacancies on the following websites: www.education.guardian.co.uk, www.tefl.com, www.tesjobs.co.uk, www.ydelta.free.sp, www.tesol-spain.org, www.bilc.co.uk, www.elfweb.com, www.developingteachers.com, www.eslemployment.com, www.englishclub.com (a site for English as a second language, with information and job offers); www.expatriatecafe.com (devoted to teaching English in Spain), www.madridteacher.com (set up by English teachers in Madrid, it lists job opportunities and has information for teachers), www.infojobs.net (in Spanish but very useful – go to 'educacion-formacion', the region you prefer, and under 'palabra' type INGLES), www.alliancesabroad.com (includes a programme for teaching English in Spain while learning Spanish) and www.spaintutor.com (puts English tutors and students of English in touch with each other).

IT

Those with qualifications and experience in IT should find no difficulties in obtaining employment in Spain. See in particular www.tecnoempleo.com.

Journalism

A number of English-language journalists operate out of Spain. English-language publications in Spain pay only very low rates, and accordingly foreign journalists in Spain make most of their earnings elsewhere, with many also teaching English as a foreign language to supplement their earnings. Spanish VAT is not strictly payable on contributions to magazines, though some publications prefer contributors to charge it.

General websites in English

www.europa.eu.int/jobs/eures
www.webseurope.com
www.exposure-eu.com
www.elsunnews.com
www.eurojobs.com
www.jobpilot.es (in English)
www.britishchamberspain.com – jobs selection worth looking at
www.spainexpat.com – a very useful site for links to many
different sites including job websites
www.segundmano.es – a Madrid newspaper, published on
Monday, Wednesday and Friday. It has a wide range of classified
advertisements. While the papers is in Spanish, you will find
and can place ads in English.
www.overseasjobs.com for overseas employment
www.surinenglish.com – good selection of jobs, especially on the
Costa del Sol
www.wemploy.com (English and Spanish). This company
specializes in finding work for expatriates on the Costa del Sol
and Costa Blanca.
www.absolute-marbella.com – small selection of jobs on the
Costa del Sol
www.marbellaguide.com – selection of jobs on the Costa del Sol
www.costadelsolnews.es – small selection of jobs on the Costa
del Sol
www.costablanca-news.com – small selection of jobs on Costa
Blanca
www.spainview.com – information site for freelance journalists
www.spanish-living.com – includes a selection of jobs, also
property and rentals
www.e4s.co.uk – specializes in employment for students in UK
and abroad. Carry out a job search for 'abroad'.
www.expatexchange.com – a selection of jobs
www.escapeartist.com – a selection of jobs and also information
and resources for living in Spain

www.tbs.com.es – website for *The Broadsheet*. Ads for Madrid, Catalonia, Andalusia, Valencia and Murcia, including rentals and some jobs

www.costadealmeria.co.uk – This is an information and community website, and gives details of property services, local newspapers, schools and rentals. It has a link to a local paper, *The Advertiser*, which has a selection of jobs mainly in bars and restaurants.

www.justlanded.com – some jobs

www.RecruitSpain.com – a recruitment company helping predominantly UK candidates find employment on the coast

www.tecnoempleo.com – lists jobs in IT and telecommunications

Websites in Spanish

Instituto Nacional de Empleo: www.inem.es

Ministry of Labour and Social Affairs: www.mtas.es

www.trabajo.org – one of Spain's largest employment organizations

www.infojobs.net

www.abctrabajo.com

www.monster.es – one of Spain's most used sites for jobs. In Spanish, but you can search instead under www.jobsearch.monster.co.uk. Look under 'Search Europe' and go to the region of Spain that interests you.

http://www.segundamano.es – popular Spanish site for a good range of jobs. There are also ads in English for teachers of English. Go to '*trabajo*' on left-hand side of the homepage and look under '*secciones*'.

www.infoempleoes – includes job advertisements and information on training, education and grants

www.todotrabajo.com – job vacancies and advice

www.tecnoemplecom – IT and telecommunications

Working on the black market (*economica sumergida*)

There are large numbers of foreigners and Spaniards working illegally in Spain, especially in construction, farming and various service industries, notably tourism. As with other forms of tax abuse, the Spanish authorities have for some time been enforcing the law, and fines have been imposed on numerous employers and indeed employees. Employees working illegally have no rights to health cover or other benefits provided by the State.

Once you have your job offer

If you are offered a job, ensure that you understand the terms of the contract before signing it. Check about relocation expenses, arrangements for accommodation, and what documentation you will require to open a bank account into which your salary can be paid. Once you have obtained employment, your employer should register you with the social security authorities. It is illegal to work in Spain without being registered, and your employer can be fined upwards of €3,000 for failing to register you. The social security authorities will send you a health card (*tarjeta sanitaria*). Your dependants will be covered under your registration. Non-EU citizens must ensure that they obtain a *tarjeta comunitaria*, or permit, at the local *Delegado de Trabajo*, or a police station. You will need your contract of employment, passport, social security card, a medical certificate (which is available from a medical centre and simply states that you have no contagious diseases) and four passport-sized photographs. The permit is issued for one year, after which it should be renewed every five years. Along with the permit you will be given a tax identification number.

Income tax

The vast majority of employees in Spain do not need to complete a tax return, which is generally only required for those earning above a certain limit. Instead the authorities send employees an assessment of their tax liability each year, and their tax liability is then met by deductions made by their employers from their salaries, with any (usually minor) adjustments made at the end of April each year.

Your social security contributions

The earnings threshold for social security contributions is around €550 a month. The contributions for an employee on that level of earnings are based on a little under 30 per cent of salary. Most of this contribution is paid by the employer. A salaried worker needs to have had contributions paid into the system for 35 years before becoming entitled to the full state pension.

The contract of employment, your rights and obligations

Traditionally Spanish law has provided considerable protection for employees, including in relation to redundancy and dismissal. In recent years the level of protection has been lowered to increase the flexibility in the labour market. Most new employment contracts are now short-term contracts under which employees receive little employment protection. Indeed the Economic and Social Committee of the European Union has called on Spain to reduce the number of temporary work contracts issued. Most people under 25 are employed on such contracts of one year's duration. Employers are entitled to offer subsequent one-year contracts to such employees, up to a maximum of three years. After that the employer must either offer a permanent position, or dismiss the employee, which it can do without any financial penalty, providing it does so within the three-year period.

The contract of employment (*contrato de trabajo*)

An employee should generally either be aged 18 or above or have the consent of his or her parents or guardian. In Spain a contract of employment does not have to be in writing: an oral agreement is sufficient. However, the law requires that certain contracts be in writing. These are contracts under which the employee is essentially receiving practical work experience or training, contracts for specific purposes, part-time and fixed-term contracts, contracts under which the employee works at home, and contracts for employees taken on in Spain for Spanish companies abroad.

If a contract does not state its duration, as may be the case with an oral contract for example, Spanish law assumes that it is of indefinite duration (and hence fully protected), unless there is evidence to the contrary.

Even for contracts of employment for an indefinite duration, employers often insist on a probationary period. To be effective in reducing the employer's obligations this must be recorded in writing, and must be for no more than two months (six months for technical personnel). During the probationary period the employer (or the employee) is entitled to terminate the contract without giving any reason, and without any period of notice (unless the contract states otherwise). While on probation employees are entitled to the same rights and subject to the same obligations as if they were part of the permanent work force. The period of probation counts towards their length of service.

Protection provided by Spanish law

Spanish labour law provides substantial protection for permanent employees. Should your employer wish to make any of the changes below, you should seek the immediate advice of a trade union representative, or obtain advice from some other appropriate source. There are special regulations governing certain categories of employment, including professional sports people, disabled people with a recognized invalidity of 33 per cent or more who carry out their work in special employment centres, and company directors who in reality own their company. Similarly there are separate rules relating to artists, commercial representatives who do not work on their employer's premises and are not subject to their employer's hours of work, seafarers and dockworkers. Household domestic employees are also governed by different rules (for example, those who work by the hour are entitled to a minimum of €3.59 per hour worked, without any further payment for holidays or the 'extra' two months – see below).

An employer is entitled to make **changes to the employment contract**, providing such changes are justified and the employer complies with the requirements of Spain's employment legislation. If an employer wishes a worker to carry out duties of a lower category it must continue to pay the employee the same salary. On the other hand, if an employer requires an employee to carry out duties of a higher category for more than six months in a year, or eight months in two years, the employee is entitled to request a promotion.

As to **relocation**, Spanish law provides that for a transfer requiring a change of residence, or when there is a temporary move lasting for more than 12 months in a three-year period, the employer must give the worker 30 days' notice of the move. The employer is also required to compensate the employee for the costs incurred. Employees are not obliged to accept the change, and can instead elect to terminate the contract, in which case they are entitled to receive 20 days' compensation for each year worked (up to a maximum of 12 monthly payments).

In relation to other significant changes in the contract involving remuneration, working hours, timetable and shift patterns, and work performance, an employer is obliged to give employees 30 days' notice of the change and pay compensation for any costs incurred. Again, employees are not obliged to agree, and can chose to leave, in which case they are entitled to receive 20 days' compensation for each year of their employment (subject to a maximum nine monthly payments).

The Spanish state guarantees payments to workers, including compensation for dismissal or termination of their contract of employment, and wages still owing when an employer becomes insolvent or bankrupt or enters into an arrangement with creditors.

The minimum wage (*salario minimo interprofesional*)

Spanish law provides for a minimum wage (SMI). It is unlawful for employers to pay less. From 1 January 2006 the SMI for all workers was €540 per month (about €18 per day). This daily rate does not include Sundays or holidays. The SMI for part-time employment is pro rata. There are also General Wages Councils in various sectors of the economy that fix adequate salary levels for different groups of workers.

Remuneration

Employees must be paid at intervals not exceeding one month, and be given a clearly itemized payslip. The employer is required to deduct tax and social security contributions. Salary is usually paid by way of 12 monthly payments. In addition, employees receive at least two extra payments per annum, one at Christmas and the other generally in the summer. Entitlement to these additional payments, known as *pagas extraordinarias* (although in fact they are not exceptional, as the name suggests, but conventionally paid) should be provided for in the contract of employment. Casual or temporary workers who have been employed by the same employer for less than 120 days are entitled (apart from the minimum daily wage) to a proportionate part of the payment for Sundays and public holidays. They also receive the two additional payments equivalent to 30 days' salary. This is subject to a minimum of about €25.50 per day.

The average monthly salary is about €1,600. A professional in IT can expect to earn a little over twice this amount.

Working time

Spanish law lays down a number of stipulations about working time. The maximum working week is limited to an average of 40 hours per week over a 12-month period. Employees should not normally work in excess of nine hours per day, except where this has been agreed as part of a collective agreement. Employees younger than 18 may not work for more than eight hours per day. Working time must be distributed fairly evenly throughout the year, unless a more irregular distribution has been agreed as part of a collective agreement.

Workers must receive at least 12 hours' rest between one working day and the next, and a minimum weekly rest of one and a half days of uninterrupted rest (two uninterrupted days for those under 18). When a working day exceeds six hours, workers must be given a rest period of at least 15 minutes. Employees aged less than 18 must receive a 30-minute break once a working day exceeds four and a half hours.

Women workers receive up to one hour off work for feeding a child under nine months of age (this time can be taken by the father instead, if both parents are working). Both men and women have an entitlement to a reduction in their work time by between one third and one half if they have direct responsibility for a child under six or a disabled person or member of their family in one of a prescribed set of circumstances.

The law provides that overtime is voluntary, unless it is the subject of an agreement to the contrary, or is to carry out emergency work. Overtime is limited to 80 hours per year. Employees should be paid an additional 40 per cent for overtime, with double time on Sundays and statutory holidays. Employees under 18 may not carry out overtime at night.

In Spain the working day is generally from 9.30 am to 1.30 pm and 4.30 pm to 7.30 pm. Foreign businesses and a growing number of Spanish companies expect their staff to work from 9 am to 6 am with an hour for lunch. The basic normal working week is 40 hours, and there is entitlement to one month's holiday in addition to 14 statutory holidays.

Holidays

Employees are entitled to a minimum of 30 calendar days of holiday each year. This cannot be replaced by a financial payment. Employers are required to give employees at least two months' notice before the dates allocated for time off. Disputes about the timing of holidays can be resolved by application to the courts. There are up to 14 public holidays a year, including Christmas Day, New Year's Day, 1 May (Labour Day) and 12 October (the Spanish National Day). Public holidays that naturally fall on a Sunday are moved to the Monday. The autonomous regions have a power to replace some of the public holidays (save those listed above) with public holidays of their own.

When a public holiday falls on a Tuesday or a Thursday, employers often declare the previous or subsequent day a holiday also, thereby giving employees a long weekend.

Retirement and pensions

Relatively few Spanish employers offer a pension scheme over and above the state pension. Payments to a company pension are tax-deductible up to a maximum of about 10,000 euros per year (though the limit is higher for older employees). There is no compulsory retirement age.

Travel expenses

Travel expenses to and from an employee's work place are deductible against tax.

Leave

Employees are entitled to paid time off for marriage (15 days) and the birth of a child (two days). The same applies to a death, accident or serious illness or hospitalization of a blood relative or relative by marriage up to the second degree (two days, or four if the employee needs to travel), moving house (one day) and time for unavoidable public duties (such as jury service).

Sickness leave

Employees are protected when they are unable to work and need medical care as a result of an illness or accident, whether or not it is work-related. To benefit when suffering from a common illness the employee must have paid 180 days' contributions during the five years immediately prior to taking absence due to illness. Sickness benefit is payable for up to 12 months only, with a possibility of a six-month extension.

Maternity and paternity leave

A woman is entitled to maternity leave of up to 16 consecutive weeks, with an additional two weeks for each child after the first in the case of multiple births. A mother must take six of these weeks immediately after the birth, but can chose when to take the other 10 weeks. If both parents work they have the right to elect for the father to take some of this time off after the birth. There are similar provisions covering adoption and fostering.

Employers receive various reductions in their social security contributions when employees are taken on to replace women on maternity leave.

Extended leave of absence

Workers who take an extended leave of absence, and who have been employed by an organization for at least one year, have a right to priority if they wish to return to work, should a vacancy arise, over a period of between two and five years. Employees are permitted to take extended leave to care for members of their family. This is for up to three years for each child, including adopted and fostered children. There is also a right to extended leave of absence to look after a blood relative or relative by marriage (up to second degree) who is unable to look after him- or herself or to work. This is limited to one year. Employers receive reductions in their liability for social security contributions for staff taken on to cover for those taking leave to care for family members.

Redundancy

If an employer wishes to make an employee redundant on economic grounds or because of a material change in the business, it must adopt the procedure prescribed by law. The employer has to make the case for a redundancy to the employment authorities by presenting a restructuring plan, and the employee must be given the opportunity to respond to the employer's case for dismissal. The employee may only be dismissed if the plan is approved by the employment authorities. If dismissed, the employee is entitled to 20 days' salary for each year of employment, up to a maximum of 12 months' salary.

Dismissal

An employer can dismiss a worker for continued absences (even if justified) and/or poor performance, but is required to pay compensation equal to 20 days' salary for each year of service, up to a maximum of 12 months' salary. An employee who is dismissed and who wishes to challenge the employer's action has the right to invoke a conciliation process, and subsequently (if necessary) to bring a claim before the Social Court. Requests for conciliation should be made within 20 working days of the dismissal. Only Sundays and public holidays are excluded for the purposes of calculating this time limit. The time limit is very short, and accordingly advice should be sought from a trade union representative, lawyer or other competent adviser as soon as possible after dismissal, or beforehand if dismissal is threatened or anticipated.

Efforts are made initially to reach a compromise and to settle the employee's claim. If no agreement is reached, the employee may bring a claim to the Social Court. This should be done as a matter of urgency, as the time limit is 20 days *from the dismissal*. The application can be lodged by the employee or by a lawyer. If an agreement is reached, the employer and employee must both abide by it. If either party breaches the agreement the other may bring legal proceedings to enforce the agreement.

An employer that is found to have unfairly dismissed an employee is liable to pay damages amounting to the pay the employee would have received, from the date of the dismissal to the date of the final hearing. It must also pay damages for future losses, consisting of 33 days' salary per year of employment, up to a maximum salary equivalent to three years and six months (for someone with over 35 years' service).

The law provides for lower levels of compensation for those in positions of management, though in practice employment contracts for higher-paid staff often contain a provision for enhanced levels of compensation for breach of contract, above the levels set for other employees.

The employment of women

Women receive an allowance of around €1,300 per year, and a reduction of €1,300 of income tax per year, if they have children under three years old and are self-employed or employees. Entitlement is limited to those who are registered with the social security authorities or have a corresponding mutual insurance scheme. Application is made on Form 140, available from any office of the *Agencia Tributaria* (Tax Agency), to which it must also be returned once completed.

When employing women aged over 25, employers benefit from a reduced liability for social security contributions, with the liability reduced further in the case of women over 45, and a still further reduction for those over 55. There is an additional reduction when employing a woman from an under-represented group, and also reduced liability for social security contributions for women who are self-employed.

Notwithstanding the above provisions, women still face considerable difficulty, especially in obtaining part-time work. The European Union has asked Spain to increase the number of part-time contracts, which would go some way towards reducing the marked differences in unemployment between the sexes.

Workers under 18

It is a criminal offence to employ children under 16, though an employer is still required to pay the child for any work performed. Parental consent is required for the employment of those aged between 16 and 18. Workers under 18 may not work at night (between 10 pm and 6 am), work overtime, or be engaged in any employment considered unhealthy, dangerous or requiring heavy labour.

Disabled workers

The physically and mentally handicapped are protected in Spain's Constitution. This protection has been given concrete form in the Act on the Social Integration of the Disabled. This provides for subsidies to ensure minimum levels of income and for assistance with the cost of transportation. A disabled person is defined as someone who has a disability assessed at 33 per cent or above. Employers must not directly or indirectly discriminate against disabled workers. Public authorities or commercial businesses employing more than 50 workers are required by law to allocate at least 2 per cent of their posts to disabled workers. In addition the Spanish authorities provide subsidies to employers in relation to disabled workers, reductions in social security contributions, and assistance in the provision of vocational training.

The state grants a subsidy of around €4,000 and a 70 per cent reduction in employer's social security contributions for the employment of a disabled woman aged under 45, and a 90 per cent reduction for older women. Reductions are also applicable to part-time female employees. In addition employers can apply for a payment for alterations to the employee's job and for training. The employer can also set an amount equivalent to these two subsidies against corporation tax.

Protection against sexual harassment

Employees who believe they have been subjected to harassment on the grounds of sex have a right to bring a complaint. This should be addressed to the *Instituto de la Mujer* (Institute for Women) or to the Institute's *Centros de Información de los Derechos de la Mujer* (Women's Rights Information Centres), with offices in Madrid, Santander and Seville. There is also a national 24-hour help line for women available free of charge. Advice and information are available on legal and practical issues. Tel: (within Spain) 900–191010 and 900–152152 for the hard of hearing.

Sources of advice on employment issues

Advice on employment rights and the General Wages Agreements can be obtained from trade unions and also from the Social-Labour Office, Administrative Information Sub-department, Agustinde Bethercourt, 11, 28071 Madrid (tel: +34 (0)91 553 6278)

Starting and running a business in Spain

Non-EU nationals intending to set up business in Spain must provide investment funds of at least €120,000 and create work for Spanish or other EU citizens.

There are many Britons and other Europeans in Spain who have faced financial ruin after the failure of their business projects, in many cases because of lack of planning and a refusal to appreciate that their plan was doomed to failure from the outset. Various agencies provide help and assistance in establishing a business. Prior to leaving the UK, you could contact the Spanish Embassy (Commercial Office) at 22 Manchester Square, London W1M 5AP (tel: +44 (0)20 7486 0101) and/or the Legal Department of the Spanish Embassy at 24 Belgrave Square, London SW1X 8QA. A number of government booklets are available in English, including 'A guide to business in Spain', 'Forms of business organizations'

and 'Labour legislation'. Take a look at the Spanish government
website www.investinspain.org.

The British Chamber is based in Barcelona at Calle Bruc 21,
08010 Barcelona (tel: +34(0) 933 17 32 20, e-mail enquiries to the
director Sarah-Jane Stone, britchamber@britchamber.com), but
also has representation in Madrid, Bilbao and Zaragoz. See the
chamber's website www.britishchamberspain.com and its
American equivalent www.amchamspain.com. Assistance can
also be obtained from Barclays Bank (www.barclays.es) and
Lloyds TSB Bank (www.lloydtsb.com). Barclays currently has
branches in Madrid, Barcelona, Bilbao, Seville and Valencia, and
following its recent acquisition of Banco Zaragozano it is set to
treble its customer base and branch network in Spain. Lloyds TSB
has branches in Madrid, Barcelona, the Canary Islands, Bilbao,
Marbella, Majorca, Navarra and Seville.

Once in Spain, you should contact the local Spanish Chamber of
Commerce. The main office in Madrid is *Consejo Superior de las
Camaras de Comercio Industria y Navegacion*, C/Velazquez 157, E-2802
Madrid (tel: +34 (0)91 590 6900, website www.camerdata.es). Ask
what other help and assistance is available. In some areas, chambers
of commerce run courses in English on how to set up a business.

To counter the difficulties of dealing with bureaucracy, all
provinces now have a one-stop centre for businesses (*ventanilla
unica*) at which all the documentation required for a new business
can be submitted together, and from which you can obtain advice
about administrative requirements. The address of your local
office can be found at www.ventanillaempresarial.org.

According to a recent conference in Seville, the start-up costs
for a small or medium-sized business in Spain amount to only
around €1,500, far below the European average cost of over
€5,000. Furthermore, the average time for the setting-up of a
business in Spain is one of the shortest, at an average of only 15
days. These figures however are averages, and in reality, as a
foreigner, you are likely to find that the costs and time required
are greater, although with the correct professional advice you are
likely to find it easier to set up business in Spain than, for example,
in neighbouring France.

The *gestor*

An essential source of help and advice is the *gestor*, who is well qualified to guide you through the bureaucratic nightmares and help with much of the paperwork that you will be required to complete. An aspect of life in Spain that is only just beginning to change is the seemingly limitless enthusiasm of Spanish government agencies for generating paperwork, and creating every conceivable kind of hurdle to undermine the smooth running of their daily contact with the public. Procedures which in other countries can be carried out speedily in person, or by post, telephone or over the internet, require a personal attendance, often necessitating a return journey of several hours, followed by hours of queuing at different counters, usually at opposite ends of the official building. To deal with this nightmare of administrative bureaucracy the Spaniards have created the profession of *gestor*. Licensed to advise and represent Spaniards and foreigners, he or she can greatly ease the burden of your everyday dealings with the state. The *gestor* can provide you with invaluable advice, or better still handle these procedures on your behalf. His or her fee is modest. After you have spent several days pulling your hair out, you will wonder why you did not use his or her services in the first place, and spend your time in some more worthwhile pursuit. While initially you may wish to rely on your lawyer, you should make enquiries among the expatriate community and any Spanish friends about any *gestors* they can recommend.

In recent years, some municipalities in areas with large numbers of foreign residents have set up specialist foreign departments, with staff who speak English and other foreign languages, and who can help with administrative problems. It should also be noted that many different forms are available from tobacconists, where queues are much shorter than in government buildings.

While any citizen of an EU country is entitled to live and work in Spain, a residence permit is not sufficient to enable you to start a business. A self-employed person, or *autonomo*, must also obtain a permit, as well as pay into the Spanish social security system, though on a different basis from an employee.

In order to establish yourself, you must:

▮ register at the local police station or *Delegacion de Trabajo*, taking your professional certificates, your passport, four photographs and a lease or *ecritura* for your business premises;

▮ register at the *Hacienda* and obtain a code;

▮ register at the local office of the social security authorities as a self-employed person (monthly contributions start at a little over €200 euros);

▮ obtain a licence for the opening of any business premises.

I would strongly advise that you instruct a *gestor* at the outset, as he or she is likely to save you a considerable amount of time and unnecessary stress.

You can run a business as a sole trader (*empresa individual*), in which case you are personally liable for the business's debts and loss. Alternatives include

▮ A partnership. Again, partners remain personally liable for the business's debts.

▮ A limited liability company, or *Sociedad Limitada*. This can be formed and owned by one person. If the company fails, the owners' liabilities are limited to the value of their shares in it. In practice, however, it is likely that an owner will have to give some personal guarantees, for example to the company's bank, or to its landlord if it operates from rented premises. To form a limited company a minimum share capital of €3,000 euros is required.

▮ A *Sociedad Anonima* (SA). This is equivalent to a plc (public limited company) in the United Kingdom. Liability is limited to the amount of capital each investor puts into the company. A minimum share capital of €60,000 is required.

▮ Establishing a branch of a foreign company.

You should seek legal and financial advice before deciding which option to adopt.

If you are contemplating the purchase of an existing business, insist on working in the business for a while before you sign anything, so that you can form your own views about the accuracy of the turnover figures, and learn the ropes prior to taking over the business.

Taxation of businesses

Social charges

If you are self-employed and do not employ anyone else, your social charges will be at least €200 from the outset, and can rise to a ceiling of around €2,600 per month. There are penalties for late payment. Once you employ others, your social charges will start to escalate. The employer's contributions are high. Once you have taken into account these and the additional two months' salary payable at Christmas and in the summer, the average total cost of an employee will approach nearly twice his or her base monthly salary. Remember that it is the employer's responsibility to register employees, and that employers can be fined for failure to do this. Take advice on the type of contract to offer before employing anyone. Remember that it may not be easy to dismiss an employee without having to pay compensation. A self-employed person is not entitled to unemployment benefit should the enterprise fail.

Business tax (*impuesto sobre actividades economicas/IAE*)

This is payable by all businesses with a turnover in excess of €1 million. Companies and the self-employed are required to register even if their turnover does not reach this level.

Company/Corporation Tax (*impuesto sobre sociedades/IBI*)

The principles of corporate taxation in Spain are the same as in the rest of the European Union. The standard rate is 35 per cent, but it is 30 per cent for small and medium-sized businesses, both partnerships and limited companies. A large proportion of enterprises fit this category. Businesses in the Canary Islands pay a maximum of only 5 per cent. Tax evasion is widespread, and the government is committed to making major changes to the corporate tax system.

If you decide to invest in your business by purchasing substantial assets, such as a computer system, you should note that not all the costs can be used to reduce taxable profits in the year in which they are purchased. Tax relief against the cost of such assets will be spread over a number of years. You may wish to consider leasing equipment, where tax deductions are more in line with expenditure. You should, of course, keep records of expenses in order to set them against the business's revenue.

VAT (*impuesto sobre el Valor Anadido/IVA*)

All businesses are required to register for VAT, to charge VAT at 16 per cent on all supplies of goods and services, and to account to the tax authorities for these sums every three months.

Business premises

As elsewhere, a great deal of business property in Spain is leased. Like the residential tenant, the business tenant benefits from a degree of protection under the law, including a right to the renewal of a business lease. This right is subject to exceptions and the completion of the necessary formalities, and you should take advice from a lawyer and/or *gestor*. It is likely that the landlord will restrict the kind of business activities allowable on the premises. For any business premises you will also need a *licencia de apertura*, a licence permitting you to open a business. The cost of these varies, but it can be as little as €150.

Finance

Bank finance

Having a business plan, in Spanish, is essential if you are to obtain a bank loan to finance your business. You will need to provide an assessment of the demand for your product or service, likely revenue, assets being introduced into the business, your fixed and variable costs and some cash flow forecasts. Banco Bilbao Vizcaya Argentaria (BBVA) has recently launched new fixed-rate loans for small and medium-sized businesses. As loans are at an historic low it is perhaps a good time for businesses to agree fixed rates to limit future financial costs.

State aid and other assistance

There are various subsidized loans, grants and subsidies available from the European Union and from central, regional and local government, particularly in the less prosperous regions. In addition, there are several tax incentives and allowances in the early years of a business. Five companies have together initiated a programme for promoting the use of high technologies in small and medium-sized enterprises in Spain: the Spanish bank Bankinter, Spanish Informatica El Corte Ingles (the information technology subsidiary of Spanish retailer El Corte Ingles), US computer maker IBM, Spanish software developer SP and Spanish telecommunications company Telefonica. The initiative is aimed at companies with 1–250 employees and an annual turnover of €40 million or less (which includes 95 per cent of all Spanish companies). The scheme provides software, hardware and telecommunications technologies.

Insurance

It is mandatory for businesses to have insurance cover for their vehicles, health insurance for their employees and property insurance. The notification period for claims is very short.

For further information on establishing a business in Spain contact UK Trade and Investment, Kingsgate House, 66–74 Victoria Street, London SW1E 6SW (tel: +44 (0)20 7215 5000) or take a look at the websites www.uktradeinvest.gov.uk and www.ukinspain.com.

3 France

The labour market in France

France has experienced substantial influxes of economic migrants over the last few years, not only from North Africa but also from Spain and Portugal. Indeed the Portuguese far outnumber the Britons in France. For the most part the newcomers are carrying out low-paid blue-collar work, and accordingly wages in unskilled work are low and jobs can be difficult to obtain. In addition, the opportunities for English-speakers to teach their mother tongue are rather more limited in France than in many of the other countries discussed in this book.

The unemployment office: *L'Agence Nationale pour L'Emploi* (ANPE)

In addition to consulting the EURES website (see page 4), job seekers should visit their local ANPE office. Indeed, those wishing to receive UK Jobseeker's Allowance while in France must register here. This is the most common means of obtaining information about job vacancies. As an EU citizen you are entitled to the same degree of advice and assistance as a French citizen. This can include not only help in finding employment, but also assistance in selecting appropriate training courses and advice on how to set up your own business. Practical assistance includes providing you with access to a telephone booth for calling potential employers free of charge, access to the internet and to a photocopier, and access to a computer to prepare your CV. In some centres you can consult reference books and company listings. You can locate your local ANPE offices by consulting Yellow Pages (*Les Pages Jaunes*) under *Administration du travail et de l'emploi*. Your first interview with an ANPE adviser will include the preparation of a *projet d'action personalisé* (PAP), a plan of action aimed at helping you find employment.

The job advertisements in the ANPE office, and indeed in the French media, often require *bac*, *bac*+2 or *bac*+3. *Bac* is short for the French *baccalauréat*, an examination taken at the end of the equivalent of the British sixth form. The figure indicates that applicants must have at least that number of years of higher education. Unemployment benefit in France is administered by ASSEDIC (*L'Association pour l'Emploi dans l'Industrie et le Commerce*, www.assedic.fr).

Employment agencies

There are numerous employment agencies in France with shop windows advertising temporary positions. You will find them listed under *Intérim* in the Yellow Pages. The largest include Manpower (www.manpower.fr) and Adecco (www.adecco.fr). Others include ADIA France (www.adia.fr) and Best-Intérim (www.best-interim.fr). Take a look a the various agencies' websites, and also www.officielinterim.com, before sending them a CV and telephoning to make an appointment. These agencies are worth consulting even though initially they can only offer you a temporary position. Such a post at least enables you to gain the experience or the reference that you might need to apply for other posts, and indeed might lead directly to permanent employment with the same employer. Temporary staff are entitled to the same benefits as permanent employees. This includes a '13th month' salary, lunch vouchers and travel subsidies. When the temporary contract comes to an end, employees should be paid a sum equal to 10 per cent of their gross salary to date, with an additional amount to cover accrued paid holidays.

Other sources of information

The business directory Kompass is definitely worth consulting (see www.kompass.fr), as are the sites www.europages.com, www.bottin.fr and www.euridile.inpi.fr. American Chambers of Commerce publish a trade directory and database for France which provides information on US subsidiaries operating in France. This costs around £100, and can be purchased from any US Chamber of Commerce or from the website www.americansabroad.com. It is also worthwhile consulting the websites of the American Chamber of Commerce in France (www.amchamfrance.org), the Franco-British Chamber of Commerce (www.francobritishchambers.com), and the British Chamber of Commerce for the French Riviera (www.bccriviera.com).

The media

There are a considerable number of English-language news-papers and magazines, and also websites such as those under the umbrella of www.angloinfo.com, that regularly contain a small number of job advertisements. In the national French press, job advertisements appear in *Le Figaro* on Mondays, and for higher-paid jobs in *Le Monde* on Mondays and Tuesdays. The specialist magazines include *Carrières et Emplois*, which is published each Wednesday. Contrary to the position in the United Kingdom, advertisements rarely give much indication about the salary offered. On the Riviera the English-language radio station Riviera Radio (www.rivieraradio.mc) has a regular job spot, though this is dominated by jobs in the yachting industry and domestic service.

Sending unsolicited letters of application

It should be noted that the French are rather more formal than the Anglo-Saxons. You should begin your letter with *Monsieur, Madame, Monsieur le Directeur* or *Madame la Directrice*. The ending should also be formal, such as *Je vous prie de croire Monsieur, à l'assurance de mes sentiments distingués* ('yours faithfully'). You should type your name underneath your signature. I recommend that you buy a specialist book with precedent letters of application and guidance on how best to present your CV and set out your correspondence. They are invariably available on the bookshelves of the larger French supermarkets. For further guidance on writing to potential employers see Chapter 1 on the European Union.

Having your qualifications recognized

For detailed information on this topic see Chapter 1. The contact details relating to France are:

Mme Françoise Profit, directrice ENIC-NARIC France
Centre international d'études pédagogiques
(CIEP/International Centre for Pedagogic Studies)
ENIC-NARIC France CIEP 4 rue Danton 75006 Paris
Phone: +33 (0)1 55 55 04 28
Fax: +33 (0)1 55 55 00 39
E-mail: enic-naric@ciep.fr
www.ciep.fr/enic-naricfr/

Specific job sectors

Teaching

There are a number of international, British and American schools in France, mainly in Paris, the largest cities and on the Riviera. Details of the schools can be obtained from the English Language Schools Association France (tel: +33 (0)1 45 34 04 11 or by e-mail: elsa.france@wanadoo.fr). This is a non-profit-making association of schools that offer advanced programmes of study in English. The association's website is at http://perso.wanadoo.fr/elsa.france. Although there is a section on job opportunities, this is not in current use. Information on schools can also be obtained from the British Council and on the website www.ydelta.free.fr/school.htm.

Job vacancies are advertised in the *Times Educational Supplement* (www.tesjobs.co.uk), and on the website of the European Council of International Schools (www.ecis.org).

Teaching English

There are many language schools in France, especially in Paris but also on the French Riviera. Language schools are listed in each department's Yellow Pages under *Cours de Langues* (see also www.pagesjaunes.fr). The French are reluctant to employ native English speakers to help their children at school as they believe they are not familiar with the school curriculum, which has a heavy emphasis on grammar and is rather dry.

Language assistants

For information on this topic see page 11. If you are already living in France, contact CIEP, tel: +33 (0)1 45 07 60 80 and see www.cief.fr.

Bilingual and legal secretaries

One agency that is well worth contacting for jobs in this field is Dorothy Danahy Legal (+33 (0)1 47 20 13 13; www.dorothydanahy.com) which has a number of prestigious clients in Paris.

Au pairs and childminding

Many boards in supermarkets and shopping centres have notices from those seeking childminders, or those offering to look after children. The websites www.aufeminin.com and www.mababysitter.com also have advertisements as well as general information. Those taking on childminders must either pay for a taxi or accompany them home. Childminders can expert to earn about €7–8 an hour. See also page 15.

Working from home

Those working from home receive a 50 per cent tax deduction. No tax is payable on the first €12,000 of earnings. In addition there is a further tax-free allowance of €1,500 per dependant. A considerable number of those working at home are engaged in telemarketing. For further information consult the websites www.bva.fr and www.sosfres.fr, or the *Syndicat du marketing téléphonique et médias électroniques* (tel: +33 (0)8 92 68 68 72).

Seasonal work

There are very good guides produced by two major French trade unions for those looking for or already engaged in seasonal work: *Ma saison en poche: le guide des saisonniers* published by the *Conféderation Générale du Travail* (CGT), and *Jobs et saisonniers: vos droits ne sont pas en vacances* by the *Conféderation Française Démocratique du Travail* (CFDT). The unions' respective websites are at www.cgt.fr and www.cdft.fr. French sites worth consulting for seasonal work are www.jobalacarte.com, www.adecco.fr www.jobsaison.com, www.studyrama.com, and www.manpower.fr.

For those intent on a summer job on the Riviera, the ANPE and the *Centre Régional Information Jeunesse* (CRIJ) have combined to produce a guidebook to assist you. Job seekers can contact advisers via ANPE, from 9 am to 4.30 pm Monday to Thursday, and 9 am to 1 pm Friday (tel: +33 (0)4 93 97 90 00). In addition to the national ANPE website (www.anpe.fr) the CRIJ has a useful website at www.crij.org/nice. The book can be obtained by contacting the Nice office of CRIJ on tel: +33 (0)4 93 80 93 93. The information contained is quite wide-ranging, including the hospitality and leisure industry, and harvesting.

As one might imagine there are large numbers of vacancies working in hotels and restaurants. Take a look at the websites www.soshotellerie.com and www.lechef.com. Employers are required to provide summer workers with meals. Busy restaurant owners are often prepared to take on those who just turn up looking for work, though be sure to avoid the busiest times. There are many potential openings over the summer for drivers and motorcycle riders, ranging from chauffeurs to bus drivers to pizza deliverers. Major employers who are keen to fill posts over the summer include Carrefour, SNCF, La Poste, the larger banks and

Escota (to operate its motorway toll booths while staff are on annual leave – see www.escota.fr). Supermarkets and hyper-markets also need to take on temporary staff. They are listed under *Centres commerciaux et grands magasins* and *Supermarchés et hypermarchés* in the Yellow Pages. You will need to make enquiries at least six months beforehand.

Those interested in working with children and young adults can find employment working in one of France's many *Colonies de vacances*, or holiday resorts. Those with a pertinent qualification such as the BAFA (*Brevet d'Aptitude aux Fonctions d'Animateur*) have the best prospects of being taken on. This is only open to those over 16. Candidates have to participate in a four-week training course costing around €900. Those who secure employment receive a rather paltry €17 or so a day, though board and lodging are included. It is worth enquiring of the local *Direction Regional Jeunesse et Sport* whether it will meet the cost of the training course.

Holiday centres also recruit those with medical or nursing training as *assistants sanitaires.* Completion of a first year of training might be sufficient to enable you to apply. Those who have completed their training might consider applying for a temporary position in a hospital. You can expect the work to be demanding, since the absence of medical and nursing staff on annual leave coin-cides with a heightened demand for health and medical services in holiday areas. For the same reason hospitals also need to recruit seasonal staff to work as porters, kitchen staff and maintenance personnel. There is a website that specializes in the recruitment of temporary staff for health services: www.quickmedicalservice.fr.

There are also numerous unskilled and semi-skilled staff required to work in campsites and holiday villages. Local police forces often take on recruits to patrol beaches and seaside resorts. It is always worth making enquires at *Mairies* to see what oppor-tunities there are in the locality, and what temporary staff the local government intends to take on over the summer. Useful websites for those wanting to work with children or in the open air include www.ucpa.com (see under *recrutement*), www.zanimateurs-fous. com, www.animjobs.com and www.clubmed-jobs.com.

Late summer and early autumn herald the start of the harvest, and a huge though short-lived demand (little more than a month) for hard labour. For information about this work see the website of the *Association Nationale pour l'Emploi et la Formation en Agriculture* (www.anefa.org). Potential employers can also be found in the Yellow Pages under *Agriculture: approvisionnement et collecte, Arboriculture et production de fruits* and *Coopératives agricoles*. Grape picking pays about €35 a day, with food and basic accommodation provided. Those harvesting the grapes work hard – up to nine hours per day, sometimes more – for seven days a week over two weeks. One website where you will find short-term work advertised, though usually only in return for board and lodging, is www.wwoof.org.

There are far less strenuous posts available as guides in cathedrals, châteaux and other historic sites and museums. These are difficult positions to find, not least because there is no central agency to apply to. Considerable effort is required to make application to individual sites. You can narrow your search down by choosing an area and contacting the main tourist offices. (For contact details of tourist offices see www.tourisme.gouv.fr.)

Further information

The most useful official sources of information relating to employment rights and training courses are www.emploi-solidarite.gouv.fr, www.droitsdesjeunes.gouv.fr and www.legifrance.gouv.fr. Recruitment websites include www.apec.asso.fr, www.cadresonline.com, www.rebondir.fr (which also produces a regular magazine), www.jobpilot.net, www.emploiregions.com, www.emploi.org, www.action-emploi.net and www.jobalacarte.com.

The black market

Employers in the construction industry, service industries and farming regularly employ tens of thousands of illegal workers, thereby evading the high levels of social security contributions in France. The penalty for those caught, both employers and employees though particularly the former, are severe. Employers risk fines of up to €30,000, not to mention the threat of imprisonment. Employees can also be fined, but may be able to bring a claim for damages against an offending employer.

Employee rights and obligations

In recent years the French authorities have introduced steps to counter racial and sexual discrimination, and to force employers in the public sector to take on more handicapped employees. New measures have been introduced to counter the discrepancy in pay between men and women, and to monitor the disadvantages faced by different ethnic minorities. The state operates various employment creation schemes aimed at different categories of worker, such as new entrants to the labour market, the long-term employed and those living in the less prosperous parts of the country. To encourage job mobility the government will make a payment called *l'aide à la mobilité géographique* of up to nearly €2,000 a year (free of any tax or social security contributions) to workers who live more than 25 km from their workplace, or have to take a journey of more than one hour.

Contracts of employment

These can be either for fixed periods of up to nine months (*contrats à durée déterminée* or CDD) or more usually permanent (*contrats à durée indéterminée* or CDI). Once a trial period of up to one month has been completed, a CDD can only be terminated if the employer follows the procedures in the Labour Code. Employers are permitted to offer fixed-term contracts for temporary employment only, or to cover for a member of staff who is on maternity leave. A fixed-term contract can be extended, but not beyond a maximum duration of 18 months, and must be in writing. If the contract does not state why the employment is only for a limited period, the employer will be stuck with a permanent appointment. Temporary workers, and also agency workers, receive a supplemental payment at the end of their contract equal to 10 per cent of the total gross salary they have been paid, and a similar payment in lieu of paid holidays.

Le contrat de professionalisation

To take on an employee under a *contrat de professionalisation* an employer must offer either a permanent contract of employment, or a fixed-term contract of 6 to 12 months. Between 15 and 25 per cent of the employee's time must be spent participating in training courses. The contract can be renewed once, though it can also be renewed should the employee fail a test or examination, or be unable to work due to illness or accident. Employees under 21 are paid only 55 per cent of the minimum wage (*le* SMIC), though those with a *bac professionnel* or similar qualification are paid 65 per cent of the SMIC. Workers aged 21 to 25 receive 70 per cent (without a *bac* or similar qualification) or 80 per cent (with a *bac* or similar qualification) of the SMIC. A major advantage for employers is their reduced liability to pay social security contributions for those employed under such training contracts.

Le contrat nouvelles embauches

This contract was introduced to encourage small businesses with up to 20 employees to take on staff, by making it easier to lay off employees should their workforce requirements change. These are permanent contracts, and are identical to the ordinary CDIs save that in the first two years of the contract, an employer can terminate the contract simply by notifying the employee by registered letter with *avis de réception*. The employer does not have to give any justification for doing this. It must give two weeks' notice from the end of the first month to the end of the sixth month of employment, and thereafter one month's notice, and pay the employee compensation for holidays not yet taken and a sum equal to 8 per cent of the total gross salary paid to the employee during the contract. This latter payment is tax-free and is not subject to any social security contributions. After two years the contract automatically becomes a standard CDI.

Other contracts subsidized by the state

Le contrat jeunes en entreprise is limited to those aged 16 to 22 with few or no qualifications. This is a permanent contract in which the employer receives a substantial subsidy over three years. It must pay the employee at least the national minimum wage. *Le contrat initiative emploi* (CEI) is for the long-term unemployed over 25, or those with dependent children. Candidates must have been out of work for at least 18 out of the previous 36 months, or 12 out of the last 18 in urban areas. The contract can be either permanent or for a fixed term of from one to two years. Again the employer receives a substantial subsidy, and in some cases the employee is entitled to continue to claim unemployment benefit. *Le contrat insertion RMI* is designed for those who have been paid supplementary benefit (RMI), or some other benefits for at least six months and who face difficulties in obtaining work. The contract must be for at least six months. The employer is paid a subsidy equivalent to the supplementary benefit paid to a single person.

Seasonal contracts and part-time contracts

Seasonal contracts, used primarily in agriculture and tourism, must be in writing and for less than eight months. Unlike other temporary contracts there is no 'bonus' paid at the end of the contract. Part-time contracts must also be in writing. Employees must work for a minimum of 60 hours per month to be entitled to social security cover.

Le chèque emploi service

This is used by employers of domestic staff, gardeners or those who look after or educate their children in their homes. The employees must not work for one employer for more than eight hours per week, but can work for several employers up to 40 hours per work. There is no written contract of employment. Instead the employer obtains a 'cheque book' from a bank or a post office, and sends a form with his or her bank details to the *Centre National de Traitement de Chèque Emploi Service Social* (CNICES). The CNICES will then deduct security contributions for the employee from the employer's bank account. The employer 'pays' a cheque to the employee, and sends a notification to CNICES. The latter will then send a pay slip to the employee. The employer benefits from a reduction in his or her personal tax bill equivalent to half the amount paid to the employee, and may be entitled to an exemption from paying social charges.

Conditions of employment

Salary and hours of work

Gross salary is termed *le salaire brut*. *Le salaire net* is net salary after deduction of social contributions of 20–25 per cent. The minimum wage in France is presently a little over €1,150 a month. This is based on a 35-hour week, at an hourly rate of €7.61. Those in semi-skilled jobs must receive at least 25 per cent more, and skilled workers 50 per cent more. An annual bonus is payable equal to one month's salary. France has a 35-hour week, although the once-rigid rules are now far more flexible. Employers can now require staff to work up to 220 additional hours (*heures supplémentaires*) a year. Employees can if they wish agree to work further hours, though they should not normally work more than 10 hours per day, or for more than six days per week. Regulations require payment for overtime to be at not less than 10 per cent above the standard hourly rate. Where there is no collective agreement governing the relationship between employer and employees, the first eight hours of overtime must be paid at 25 per cent above the standard rate, and thereafter at 50 per cent above.

Leave from work

Standard holiday entitlement is five weeks per year. Employers often require staff to have been employed for at least 12 months before they can take this leave, although this practice was declared unlawful by the European Court of Justice as long ago as 2001. In addition France has 11 public holidays. A married couple (or partners to a PACS) employed in the same company have the right to take their holidays at the same time. The French still have a strong preference for taking as much annual leave as possible during August. Accordingly, to encourage employees to take their holidays outside the normal holiday season, those who take some of their leave between 31 October and 1 May benefit from one to two days' extra annual holiday.

If someone is ill and unable to work a doctor is required to fill out a Cerfa No 10170*02. Once the employee has completed the patient's section he or she sends this (within 48 hours) to the employer and the social security scheme.

Rights in pregnancy

Once a woman is pregnant her employers must not require her to work in excess of 10 hours per day. She must not be asked to carry out difficult tasks, or to work for two weeks before the expected date of delivery, or during the six weeks after the birth. If a woman's work involves contact with chemicals or certain other products, the employer must offer her a temporary change of work. Pregnant women receive maternity benefit from the CPAM, and an additional allowance from the employer, until one month after their return from maternity leave. Expectant mothers on night shifts must be offered a change to a day shift. Where this is not practicable their contract of employment is suspended. During the suspension the woman is paid a daily allowance from the CPAM, supplemented by an additional payment from the employer.

Maternity leave consists of at least 6 weeks' leave before the estimated due date, followed by 10 weeks after the birth. Mothers who already have two dependent children may take 8 weeks' leave before the birth and 18 afterwards. Attendance at antenatal appointments can be during working hours, and must be without any deduction of salary. Similarly fathers are entitled to 3 days' leave on the birth of their child as well as paternity leave of 11 consecutive days (up to 18 for multiple births). A father must take this leave in one stretch and within four months of the birth. Fathers receive paternity leave allowance paid by the state.

Losing a job

French law requires that employers must comply with certain procedural requirements prior to dismissing an employee. The employee must first be sent by registered letter an invitation to an interview. The letter should give the employee at least five days' notice prior to the interview, to enable him or her to take advice, and to give them the opportunity of arranging for a friend to accompany him or her at the interview. The purpose of the interview is not merely for the employer to explain why it is proposing to dismiss the employee, but also for the employer to hear the employee's explanation and response. Should the employer decide that it will dismiss, it must notify the employee by registered letter, setting out in detail the reason for the decision.

There is a right of appeal to an employment tribunal (*Le Conseil des Prud'hommes*). If the Conseil determines the case for the employee, then where the employee has been employed by the employer for more than two years, and the employer has more than 11 employees, it can order the reinstatement of the employee. Failure by the employer to re-engage will make it liable to pay damages of an amount in excess of six months' salary. Those who have worked for their employer for less than two years are still entitled to bring a claim for unfair dismissal, save that there is no right to re-engagement. The tribunal can only award damages for actual loss of earnings.

Those aged under 18

Parents should note that children's earnings form part of parents' income for tax purposes and should be included on parents' tax returns. Children of 14 and above may work during school holidays of longer than 14 days. They must not work for more than half the school holiday. Further they are limited to working no more than four and a half hours at a time, with a break of at least 30 minutes. They must not work at all between the hours of 8 pm and 6 am. Children need their parents' written permission to work, and must first consult a *médecin du travail*. An employer is also required to seek the consent of the *inspection du travail* at least two weeks before a child under 16 is due to commence work. Employers are generally reluctant to jump these hurdles, and prefer not to employ children. Under-16s must be paid at least 80 per cent of the minimum wage.

Although the minimum working age is 16, teenagers between 16 and 18 must still obtain their parents' consent in writing in order to work. There is no requirement, however, for the employer to seek the permission of the *inspection du travail*. Young people must receive at least 90 per cent of the minimum wage. Their hours of work are restricted to 35 per week and 7 per day. They may not work between the hours of 10 pm and 6 am, and may not be required to work on Sundays or public holidays, save in hotels, restaurants and hospitals. Working in bars is forbidden. They must be paid at least 90 per cent of the SMIC. An employer is required by law to provide a young person with a written contract, even for a short period of employment. This must state how long the contract is to last, where the minor is required to work and the nature of the work.

Further guidance and advice

The French government has two main websites that contain information on employee rights, access to jobs, and training courses: www.emploi-solidarite.gouv.fr and www.travail.gouv.fr. It should be noted also that employees have the right to enrol for part-time or full-time training courses up to one year in duration, and in some cases longer (see www.fongecif.com). Participants are paid up to 100 per cent of their salary, as well as their training expenses. Surprisingly courses do not have to correspond with participants' current occupations, and many use this as the start of a career change, or even just for personal interest. Their contract of employment is suspended for the duration of the course, giving them the right to return to work following the completion of their studies.

Setting up a business in France

It is important to obtain expert advice from the outset. There are many sources of advice, including a number of governmental organizations, some of which also provide financial assistance. The French Chamber of Commerce in the UK (www.ccfgb.co.uk) and the French embassy (www.ambafrance.org.co.uk) both provide information in English about the creation and running of businesses in France. Guidance is also available from the American and British Chambers of Commerce in France (www.amchamfrance.org, www.francobritishchambers.com and www.bccriviera.com), as well as local chambers of commerce in France. The ANPE (*l'Agence Nationale pour l'Emploi*) holds workshops and advice sessions and also free courses in French for foreigners (see its website www.anpe.fr). The local *Chambres de Commerce et d'Industrie* (CCI) also have specialist advisers, and in some cases even organize courses in English about starting and running a business in France. Adie (*L'Association pour le développement de l'initiative économique*) has loans that it makes available to people unable to obtain bank finance (www.adie.org).

Other agencies worth consulting are *Assedic* (www.assedic.fr), *L'Agence Pour la Création d'Entrprise* (www.apce.com) and *France Active*, which provides guarantees for bank loans and other financial support and assistance to those who are unemployed (www.franceactive.org). Those out of work can obtain subsidized expert advice thanks to a scheme operated by the DDTEFP

(*Direction Départementale du Travail, de l'Emploi et de la Formation Professionnelle*). The scheme enables them to obtain advice from an *avocat, notaire* or *expert-comptable* at a cost of only €15.24 an hour. The government pays an additional €45.74 for the expert's advice.

Raising finance

It is not easy to persuade French banks to back a new venture, and it is rare that they lend more than 70 per cent of the cost of buying a business or business premises. You may find it more productive to investigate what other financial assistance might be available, and identify an accountant or business lawyer to assist you. Should you succeeded in obtaining backing from another source, a bank is more likely to provide additional funds.

If you are to persuade any government body or private organization to provide you with financial backing or guarantees you will definitely need a business plan. You must demonstrate the demand for your product or service, and produce estimated cash flow patterns showing that your business will survive the initial years. There are a host of different grants, subsidies and loans at favourable rates offered by the European Union, central, regional and local government, especially for new businesses starting up in the poorer regions. Always make contact with the local *Mairie* and *chambre de commerce* to find out what local initiatives are in place. Other organizations to contact include DATAR (www.datar.gouv.fr) and F*rance Initiative Réseau* (www.fir.asso.fr). The *Banque de Développement des Petites et Moyennes Entreprise* (www.bdpme.fr) has a number of types of loans that it makes available to assist businesses to start up or to expand. A useful source of information on financial assistance is the website www.subsidies-in-france.com. For women wishing to start a business the *Fonds de Garantie à l'Initiative des Femmes* (www.droits-femmes.gouv.fr) offers loans and loan guarantees.

There are a number of sources of financial assistance for those out of work, including tax reductions and rebates, subsidies and loans. L'Accre (*Aide aux Chômeurs Créateurs ou Repreneurs d'Entreprise*) entitles them to exemptions from social contributions for a year. Those aged 50 and over can obtain an interest-free loan of up to €6,098 from Eden (*Encouragement au développement des entreprises nouvelles*). Do not start operating your business until you have taken advice about an appropriate starting day. A short delay may enable you to increase your rights to state benefits, or enable you to postpone payment of tax. If your venture falls within the scheme *Jeune Entreprise Innovante* (JEI) you can benefit from a range of tax incentives and allowances for up to eight years. Further information on this can be found at www.impots.gouv.fr (under JEI).

Businesses starting up or relocating to any of the 41 '*zones franches*' or development zones, which were created to help disadvantaged areas, benefit from various tax exemptions over five years. They are required to recruit at least a third of their employees locally (see the information on www.travail.gouv.fr/fse).

A considerable number of Britons are now running *gîtes* in France, and a significant proportion of them have been successful in obtaining grants from *Gîtes de France*.

Business structures

There is a greater variety of structures for carrying out business in France than in the United Kingdom. The most popular with British expatriates is *l'entreprise individuelle* (EI). It is the choice of those who wish to work on their own. No capital is needed to set up the business apart from a fee of €59.19, and there are no running costs. The owner of an *enterprise individuelle* is personally responsible for all business debts, though it is now possible to protect your home from creditors by a *déclaration d'insaisissabilité* (declaration on non-seizability). This is made before a *notaire* and is registered with the *Bureau des Hypothèques* and published in the local official newspaper. If you are married you should take legal advice about your choice of matrimonial regime. The first choice of many sole traders is *la séparation des biens*. Electing this regime keeps your spouse's assets from being at risk from creditors should your business fail.

Another popular option among the British running businesses in France is *la société à responsabilité limitée* (SARL). This is a limited-liability company with at least two shareholders. There is no minimum share capital, and the liability of shareholders should the company fold is limited to the value of their shareholding. In many cases, of course, directors or shareholders will have to guarantee the company's bank accounts and bank loans to the company, and so they are by no means free of liability in the event of the company failing. The company's registered office can be a director's home, or even simply a letterbox company address with a *société de domiciliation*.

The *entreprise unipersonelle à responsabilité limitée* (EURL) is a one-shareholder limited company which requires a minimum share capital of only €1. A *société anonyme* is the equivalent of the UK plc. A minimum share capital of €37,000 is required. The *société civile immobilière* (SCI) is a structure designed for those wishing to buy, sell and manage property, and is often the choice of landlords. One advantage is that the ownership of the company (and hence of the property held by it) is easy to transfer, often with little tax liability.

Working with your spouse

There are numerous successful fledgling businesses that have been started by a husband and wife team, with perhaps one of them working only part-time in the business. You should discuss the options with an accountant or legal adviser at an early stage in your plans. Your partner could be a shareholder with you (*conjoint associé*) if you operate as a company, or an employee in the business (*conjoint salarié*) if you operate as a *entreprise individuelle* or as a limited company. The third option is as a *conjoint collaborateur* (if you operate as an *entreprise individuelle*, or as a single owner of a EURL), where the partner works for no payment but is entitled to health cover and maternity benefits. Once a *conjoint collaborateur* has worked for 10 years without payment she or he has the right to a capital sum on the eventual death of his or her partner. No inheritance tax is payable. A spouse may also receive the benefit of his or her partner's pension rights following death.

Naming and registering your business

You should ascertain from the *Institut National de la Propriété Industrielle* that the name you propose to adopt for your business is not already in use by someone else (see www.impi.fr). You must make an appointment at your local *Centre de formalités des entreprises* (CFE), where you will obtain assistance in completing a number of necessary formalities. You can find the contact details of all CFEs at www.sirene.tm.fr/annuaire.cfe. They will assist you in the preparation of the documentation required by various government agencies. You will need a certificate confirming that you have no criminal record, and also the title deeds or lease of the premises from which you will run the business. In brief, CFEs fall into three categories according to your business activity. The *Chambre de commerce et d'industrie* is responsible for retailers, shopkeepers and others in the service industry, and the *Chambre des métiers* for the building trade. Surveyors, doctors, dentists, lawyers, accountants and other members of *les professions liberales* register with the URSSAF.

On registration with your CFE you will receive a *Récépissé de Création d'Entreprise*. This includes your SIREN or business number (*K-bis*). You must wait until receipt of your *K-bis* to start operating your business. This is an extract of the entry on the *Registre de Commerce et de Sociétés* or *Répertoire des Métiers* relating to your business. You will subsequently be given a full business number or SIRET, which is the SIREN number that you received, with some further figures added. You must ensure that the SIRET is included on all your business stationery, such as invoices, estimates and receipts.

Business premises

Buying business premises is not very different from purchasing a home (see my book *The Complete Guide to Buying Property in France* (Davey, 2006)). As in the United Kingdom, however, many businesses lease their premises. Business tenants benefit from a degree of protection under French law, and have a right to renew a business lease, although there are a number of exceptions to this right that enables landlords to regain possession. A landlord who recovers his property is required to compensate the business tenant. You should note that leases usually limit the type of business activity that tenants may operate from the premises, and accordingly you may need to obtain the landlord's consent if you wish to change your business activity while remaining at the same premises.

Purchasing a business (*fonds de commerce*) is more complicated than simply purchasing or renting premises (*les murs* or *les locaux*). You may find yourself being asked to make substantial payments for the goodwill or the name of the business. It is sensible to require the vendor to allow you to work in the business for a period of time before you sign the purchase contract. This gives you the opportunity to make an assessment of the reliability of the sales figures provided by the vendor, as well as a chance to learn how the business is run.

Businesses and business properties are offered for sale by many estate agents, including British and French estate agents targeting prospective British purchasers of residential property. There are frequently advertisements in the English-language press such as *French News* and *French Property News,* and on their respective websites, www.frenchnews.com and www.french-property-news.com. A browse through a French newsagents will quickly identify the French magazines specializing in this field, though often the best source will be local newspapers.

You are entitled to carry out some work to business premises without obtaining the prior consent of local authorities, such as repairs to the shopfront or the erection of a business sign. You will, however, still need to file a *déclaration de travaux exempts de permis de construire* with the *Mairie*. If you propose to change the use of the premises you are required to obtain a *permis*. The same applies if you increase the size of the premises by more than 20 square metres. Where shop premises exceed 300 square metres you will need to obtain permission from the *préfecture*. A substantial number of Britons operate 'bed and breakfasts' in France. Provided that they have no more than five bedrooms they simply need to be registered with the local *Mairie* and with the *préfecture*. Those with more accommodation will probably need to register as hotels, which is more complicated.

Operating a business from home

Those starting a new business often do so from home, thereby keeping their expenses down and reducing travel time. You are permitted to register your business at your home address. This is true also for those in rented accommodation (at least for the first five years), though they must not receive customers or deliveries of goods to their home, and the property must be their principal residence. The position is more complex for those living in a *copropriété*. These frequently have regulations forbidding businesses from operating from the development, or restricting the type of business that may be run from there. There are additional tax allowances for people working from home, enabling them to offset one-third of certain expenses against the income of the business.

Purchasing a business franchise

A popular means of starting a business is purchasing a franchise. Often the franchise vendor has a real interest in you succeeding and, for a price, will provide you with support and guidance. Information about business franchises can be obtained from *La Fédération Française de la Franchise* (www.franchise-fff.com) and also at www.ac-franchise.com and www.observatoiredelafranchise.com.

Insurance

Employers are required as a matter of law to have insurance cover for employees, property and business vehicles. Should you need to claim you must notify the insurers. The notification periods are usually quite short.

Taxation of business income and social security contributions

Depending on the type of the business structure adopted, business owners pay either *impôts sur le revenu* (income tax) or *impôts sur les sociétés* (corporation tax). A person running an *entreprise individuelle* pays *impôts sur le revenu*; the single shareholders of an EURL have the choice of which tax to pay, but tend to choose *impôts sur le revenu*. A SARL must pay corporation tax, though in the case of a *SARL de famille*, income tax is paid.

In relation to *les impôts sur le revenu* there are three different types of tax regime: *micro-entreprises*, *régime simplifié* and *régime réel*. In short, small fledgling businesses invariably opt for the micro-system: it is far less demanding from an administrative point of view, and generally results in a lower tax bill than either of the other regimes. A fixed sum is deducted for expenditure thereby saving the need to calculate actual costs incurred. The micro regime is only available to an *entreprise individuelle* or EURL paying income tax and with a turnover of under €27,000 for commercial services, and €76,300 for businesses selling goods, that is not registered for VAT. With the other two regimes actual expenses are deducted. The main difference between them relates to the frequency with which they have to account to the authorities for the VAT charged.

Not all the purchase costs of significant business assets can be offset against income in the tax year in which they are bought: they must be spread over a number of years. In order to aid cash flow, many businesses opt to lease equipment so that deductions can be claimed fully in the years in which the expenditure is incurred. All business must keep records of their expenses, in order to justify their deduction against income for tax purposes. A skilled accountant (*expert-comptable*) is an invaluable asset when it comes to tax.

Owners of an *entreprise individuelle* or EURL, and the majority shareholders of a SARL, come under the *régime des non-salariés*. At one time employees received greater benefits under the social security system than the self-employed. This is no longer true, except in relation to unemployment benefits. Social security charges are high, though not during the first two to three years of the business, when contributions are assessed on a notional level

Garda. Wages are generally low (though supplemented by tips) and large numbers working in the tourist and leisure industry do so on the black market. In the winter months there is a substantial demand for labour in Italy's ski resorts. Potential employers worth contacting are Crystal Holidays (www.shgjobs.co.uk), PGL Travel, Darwin (www.darwinstaff.com) and Anderson Animatore.

Specific job sectors

There is a high demand for English teachers, but generally the Italians insist on candidates having graduate status, a TEFL qualification and some knowledge of the Italian language. The largest chains of language schools are those operated by Berlitz, Wall Street and Linguarama. The addresses of these and other language schools (*scuole di lingue*) are easy to locate online using www.paginegialle.it.

In the agricultural sector competition for unskilled jobs is fierce, with increasing numbers of workers arriving from the new member states of the European Union who are prepared to accept low wages and poor working conditions. Prospects of obtaining short-term work are highest during late September and most of October, when large numbers of people are required to pick grapes and apples.

There are numerous openings for au pairs. Websites worth consulting include www.aupairinternational.comk and www.euro-placements.com.

Health care

For health care you should register with the *Unita Sanitaria Locale*, or USL, taking with you form EH1C. You should then be provided with a certificate confirming your entitlement. At the USL you can obtain a list of the doctors registered under the scheme. When visiting a doctor you will be required to pay a fee that you can then recover. For medicines you will be charged either a partial or a full fee. If you are charged the full amount you can recover some of this, but will need the price tags and receipts to do this.

Social security

Once you begin working you will be required to contribute to the Italian social security system. National Insurance payments are deducted by the employer, and paid to the INPS, which administers the social security system, *il sistema di previdenza sociale*. The social security system embraces payments to the retired, disabled, sick and unemployed. Those who are unemployed in Italy are required to register with their local *Centro per Impiego* where they can also claim *indennitá di disoccupazione* (unemployment benefit).

Taxation

Italy's tax system is notoriously complex and large numbers of Italians resort to instructing an accountant or *commercialista* to advise them or to handle their tax affairs. You can obtain information from the website of the Ministry of Finance (*Ministero delle Finanze*) at www.finanze.it or your local office or *Ufficio Imposte Dirette*. You will find this listed in the telephone directory under *Ufficii Finanziari*.

The most important local Italian tax is the *Imposta Comunale Immobili* (ICI), which is a tax on the value of any property that you own, and is currently between 4 per cent and 6 per cent depending on the local authority. Charges are also made for rubbish disposal (*nettezza urbana*) and water supplies (*acquedotto comunale*). These are based on the area occupied by the property.

Employment rights

The majority of industries are subject to their own legal minimum wage. Employees receive an additional or 13th-month salary payment in December. In some sectors, however, annual salaries are divided by 14, 15 or occasionally 16, with up to four 'extra' payments.

Employees may not work in excess of 48 hours a week, though the normal working week is 40 hours. Employers are not permitted to impose compulsory overtime, and in some sectors a ban on overtime is operated. Where overtime is worked employers must pay 30–50 per cent above the standard hourly rate. Holiday entitlement is 25–30 days per year according to length of service. This is in addition to 10 days of statutory public holidays.

Accommodation

In Italy rental contracts are generally for a period of four years, though shorter and longer periods are available. You will find advertisements for properties to rent under *appartamenti da affittare* in the classified sections of newspapers. You can also find rental properties through estate agents (*agenzie immobiliari*) as they tend to handle both properties for rental and for sale.

A number of British agents have Italian properties on their books, or specialize in the Italian property market, often in association with a local agent. A particularly useful website is www.lifeinitaly.co.uk. It has links to Italian estate agents, an Italian mortgage guide and relocation experts. Other property websites include www.liguriaproperties.com and www.property-sales-italy.com. The publication *Italy Magazine* has property advertisements (see its website www.italymag.co.uk where you will find a range of information on this and other topics relating to Italy). The Italian publication *Ville & Casali* has advertisements in English as well as Italian.

A number of Italian banks are seeking to sell mortgages (*ipoteche*) to British residents and non-residents. These include the

Banca Woolwich, now taken over by Barclays (see its website www.bancawoolwich.it where it has a section devoted to prospective British property purchasers). The Italian subsidiary of the Abbey National was taken over by Banca per la Casa in 2003. It also has a section on its website in English devoted to advising foreign buyers (see www.bancaperlacasa.it).

Education

Nearly all children aged from three to five attend *scuola dell'infanzia* or nursery schools, mostly provided by the state. Compulsory primary schooling starts at age six in *scuola elementare*. At age 11 children take an examination in order to permit them to go on to secondary school.

A child's secondary education consists of two cycles. The first, or *scuola media*, is compulsory and covers the first three years of secondary education. After completing this first cycle pupils move on to upper secondary education. This is compulsory for the first year only. There are four different types of secondary schools: the *liceo classico* or classical school in which pupils study classical literature and ancient languages, or modern literature and modern languages; the *liceo scientifico* for mathematics or social sciences; the *liceo artistico* for art and music; and the *istituti tecnici* or technological institutes, of which there are five different kinds.

Higher education

There are two different kinds of universities in Italy, the *istituti universitari* and the *università politecnici*. In the former students can study a wide range of subjects, but the latter is devoted only to architecture and engineering.

Comparability of qualifications

See page 7. The contact point is:

Carlo Finocchietti, CIMEA (*Centro di Informazione sulla Mobilità e le Equivalenze Accademiche*), Fondazione Rui, Viale XXI Aprile 36
00162 Rome
Tel: +39 (0)6 8 632 1281; Fax: +39 (0)6 8 6 32 2845
Website: www.fondazionerui.it
E-mail: info@fondazionerui.it

Emergency information

Telephone 115 for the fire brigade, 118 for an ambulance, 113 for the police and 112 for the carabinieri. These calls are free.

Useful addresses

Italian Embassy
14 Three Kings Yard, Davies Street
London W1K 4EH
Tel: +44 (0)207 312 2200
Fax: +44 (0)207 499 2283
Website: www.embitaly.org.uk
E-mail: ambasciata.londra@esteri.it

Italian State Tourist Office
1 Princes Street
London W1R 8AY
Tel: 0207 408 1254
Fax: 0207 493 6695
Website: www.enit.it

The British Embassy Italy
Via XX Septembre 80a
00187 Rome
Tel: +39 (0)6 4220 0001
Fax: +39 (0)6 4220 2347
Website: www.britain.it

British Chamber of Commerce for Italy
Via Dante 12
20121 Milano
Tel: +39 (0)2 8777 98
Fax: +39 (0)2 8646 1885
Website: www.britchamitaly.com
E-mail: bbci@britcham.com

Ente Nazionale Italiano Turismo (ENIT)
Via Marghera 2
00185 Rome
Tel: +39 (0)6 49711
Fax: +39 (0)6 446 3379
Website: www.enit.it

5 Greece

Greece remains an attractive location for holidaymakers and for expatriates seeking a new life in a warm climate. The cost of living is certainly substantially lower than in the United Kingdom. EU nationals are of course entitled to work in Greece without restriction, providing they have a full 10-year EU passport. If you are in search of work, or have already obtained it, but you do not intend to stay in Greece for more than three months, you should register with the local police station within eight days of arriving. If you intend to remain for longer, you must obtain a residence permit from your nearest Aliens Department office. You will be issued with a temporary permit where your employment is expected to last for between 3 and 12 months. You should subsequently receive a full permit lasting six months. When you come to renew this you should be issued with a five-year permit.

The contact details of the offices of the Aliens Department are:

Athens: 173 Alexandras Ave – tel: +30 (0)210 641 1746
Pallini: 14 Ath Diakou St – tel: +30 (0)210 603 2980
Glyfada: 23 Karaiskaiki – tel: +30 (0)210 962 7068
Elefsina: 18 Iroon Polytechnicou St – tel: +30 (0)210 554 7427
Lavrio: 3 Damoukara St – tel: +30 (0)220 922 5265
Piraeus: 37 Iroon Polytechniou St – tel: +30 (0)210 412 4133

Unemployment is much higher than in the United Kingdom and there is more competition for unskilled employment than 10 or 15 years ago, with the arrival of many migrant workers from neighbouring Balkan countries. There are nevertheless opportunities for English speakers in jobs where the English language is a continuing advantage, such as in the tourist industry from May to

September, catering for other western Europeans, looking after the children of Greek parents keen for them to acquire a knowledge of English, and of course in language schools.

Obtaining employment

An obvious first port of call is the local office of the state employment service, the *Organismos Apasholisseos Ergatikou Dynamikou* or OAED (see its website: www.oaed.gr). Offices are listed in the local telephone directory (*tilephonikos odigos*). Additional help and information can be obtained form the national office of the European Employment Service (EURES) which is located at the OAED Head Office: EURES (SEDOC), Ethnikis Antistasis 8, 16610 A. Kalamaki (tel: +30 (0)210 994 2466 or +30 (0)210 993 5705).

Private employment agencies are illegal in Greece, though there are organizations that bear much similarity to employment agencies, covering services such as cleaning and security staff, nursing and hotel staff. You should find them listed in the *Chryssos Odigos* (or Yellow Pages) under *Grafia Evrésseos Ergassías*.

Other means of locating job opportunities

The websites and classified advertisements of the main newspapers and magazines in Greece can all be accessed via the website www.dolnet.gr. This includes several publications in English, notably *Athens News* (www.athensnews.gr). You will find various trade directories such as Kompass available for consulting in reference libraries. It is also worthwhile visiting the websites of the British and American Chambers of Commerce.

The contact details for the British Chamber of Commerce in Athens are: British Hellenic Chamber of Commerce, 25 Vas. Sophias Ave, Athens 10674 (tel: +30 (0)210 721 0361/0493, fax: +30 (0)210 7212119, website: www.bhcc.gr). For 25 euros candidates can place their CV on the website and receive a list of British companies operating in Greece. Details of British businesses can also be obtained by consulting the Chamber's directory. There is also a second branch of the British Hellenic Chamber in Northern Greece at 26 Komninon St, 54624 Thessaloniki (tel: +30 (0)2310 236 460, fax: +30 (0)2310 282 839, website: www.bhcc.gr). The website of the American Chamber of Commerce is at www.amcham.gr

There is a substantial expatriate population in Athens, and you may find fellow English speakers to be the best source of help and advice. Those in search of jobs and/or accommodation in Athens should consult the English-language *Athens News* (www. athensnews.gr) and the US website www.ads-in-greece.com. There is a network of Anglican churches in Greece, and a large international Protestant church in Athens (www.standrewsgreece.com).

Other sites of interest include www.greece.com, www. greece-athens.com, www.athensguide.com, and www. jobsabroadbulletin.co.uk

Teaching English

In addition to the various general websites covering a wide range of countries (see page 11), I would recommend that you consult the Anglo-Hellenic recruitment agency (www.anglo-hellenic.com). It promises to provide its candidates with practical support throughout the term of its appointment. Another website worth visiting is www.tesolgreece.com.

Voluntary work in Greece

The website www.gogreece.about.com contains a list of volunteer organizations operating in Greece, in fields including wildlife preservation, teaching, archaeology and construction work. There is also a link specifically to assist Australians seeking work in Greece. For work camps consult www.unaexchange.org. Other useful websites include www.teachabroad.com and www.globalvolunteers.org. In addition you can obtain voluntary work in

Greece through International Voluntary Service (IVS), Old Hall, East Bergholt, Colchester CO7 6TQ (tel: +44(0)1206 298215, fax: +44(0)1206 299043, website: www.ivs-gb.org.uk).

Employment rights

Under Greek labour law there is a maximum duration of two months for probationary periods. After satisfactory completion of that trial period, an employer is required to give the employee a regular contract of employment. The standard working week is 40 hours. There are restrictions on working overtime and on a Sunday. Employees are entitled to a minimum of four weeks' holiday after one year's employment in addition to the 11 statutory public holidays. There is currently no national minimum wage. However, there are minimum wages that apply to different employment sectors that have been the subject of collective agreements.

Finding accommodation

You will find property to rent under the heading *Enikiassis Atkiniton* in Greek newspapers. It is usual for landlords to require a deposit equivalent to two months' rent. A standard duration for a rental contract is two years. Generally rented accommodation is not difficult to find, save in Athens where rents are also substantially higher then elsewhere. You will find properties for rent listed at www.propertygr.com.

The Greeks do not have an equivalent to UK estate agencies. Greeks often enlist the assistance of a lawyer in property dealings. In the United Kingdom you will find advertisements for property in Greece in publications such as *International Property Times*. Websites to consult include www.propertygr.com, www.apropertyingreece.com and ww.realestate-greece.com.

Education

Compulsory education for children under six is in the process of being introduced area by area. There are nursery schools (*Nipiagogia*) for children from three and a half upwards. These usually take children on a part-time basis for around three to four hours a day. Children attend primary schools (*Dimotiko Scholio*) from the ages of 6 to 12. School starts at 8.15 am and finishes at 1.30 pm.

Secondary schooling is divided into lower and upper. Lower secondary schools (*Gymnasio*) cater for 12 to 15 year olds. Lessons can take place in the evenings as well as during daytime. All children follow the same compulsory curriculum consisting of maths, science, history, geography, ancient Greek literature, Modern Greek, a foreign language (usually English, but German or French are also studied), religion, domestic science, physical education and art. Physics, chemistry, biology, computing and civics are also studied in the last two years.

After completing three years in the *Gymnasio* pupils have the option of moving up to upper secondary school in the *Eniaio Lykeia* or technical schools. This is not compulsory, and also lasts for three years.

British families moving to Greece who wish to continue with an English education will find details of a number of schools primarily in Athens offering an education in English (see www.britishcouncil.gr – go to 'Education', 'UK Education in Greece' and scroll down the page to 'Nursery, Primary and Secondary Schools'). You can contact the British Council by e-mail: general.enquiries@britishcouncil.gr.

Higher education

Higher education in Greece consist of nearly 20 university institutions or *Anotata Ekpaidevtika Idrimiata* (AEIs). In addition there are around 10 technical colleges or *Technologika Ekpaidevtika Idrimiata* (TEIs), where the emphasis is more on vocational training. The Greeks have two academic terms, the first running from early October until January and the second from February to early June.

Health

European citizens should take their EHIC (European Health Insurance Card), which has replaced the old E111, with their passport to the local office of IKA (see below). You should receive an *iatrico vivliario* or health services book and be told the contact details of an IKA clinic, a doctor and a dentist listed with IKA. There is no charge for consultations or treatment. You are required to make a contribution towards the cost of investigations such as X-rays, and pay for services such as physiotherapy. If your doctor gives you a prescription, you take this with your health services book to any pharmacist listed by IKA. You are only required to pay a proportion (well under half) of the cost of prescribed medicines. Should the pharmacist charge you the full price you can obtain a partial refund, but you must retain the receipt and the prescription and the self-adhesive labels from the medicine packet, which you will need to stick to the doctor's prescription.

Social security

Social security provision is dealt with by two public bodies: IKA (health, sickness, maternity and old age benefits) and OAED (unemployment and family benefits). IKA is responsible for collecting social security contributions, and it does this by deductions from your salary. Employers should register new employees with IKA, and you should check that this is done. Social security contributions are deducted at source by your employer.

If you lose your job while in Greece you should contact the local branch of OAED, where you can obtain guidance on how to make a claim for benefits.

EU citizens can obtain advice and assistance from the international relations departments (*Tmima Diethnon Scheseon*) of both organizations:

IKA: Information Office (Citizen's Communication Office)
8 Agiou Konstantinou Str.
10241 Athens
Tel: +30 (0)210 52 34 211

OAED: Ethnikis Antistasis 8 Str.
17456 Alimos
Tel: +30 (0)210 99 89 000
Website: www.oead.gr

Qualifications equivalence

See the information on this topic on page 7. The contact details for
the Greek NARIC are:

DIKATSA, Inter-University Centre for the recognition of
Foreign Academic Titles
223 Messogion Ave
11525 Athens
Tel: +30 (0)210 675 6362/6368/6464/6494
Fax: +30 (0)210 675 6709
Website: www.hri.org/info/help/dikatsaen.htm
E-mail: dikatsa@otenet.gr

You can also obtain details from the Section for Recognition of
Professional Qualifications, Ministry of National Education and
Religious Affairs, Panepistimiou 67, 10564 Athens (tel: +30 (0)210
324 3923, website: www.srpq.gr, e-mail: srpq@otenet.gr) and OEEK
(Organization for vocational education and training), Ethnikis
Antistaseos 41, 14234 N. Ionia, Athens (tel: +30 (0)210 270 9141,
website: www.oeek.gr).

Taxation

You can obtain information on income tax, VAT and any local taxes from your local tax office (*efories*), and also from the Ministry of Finance Ypourgio Ikonomiko Tmima Diethnon Scheseon, Sina Street 2–4, 10184 Athens (tel: +30 (0)210 360 4825).

Emergency information

The telephone numbers for free emergency calls are: police 100, ambulance 166 and fire brigade 199.

Useful addresses

British Council
Filikis Etairias 17, Kolonaki Sq
10673 Athens
Tel: +30 (0)210 369 2333
Fax: +30 (0)210 363 4769
Website: www.britishcouncil.gr
E-mail: general.enquiries@britishcouncil.gr

Also at 9 Ethnikis Amynis Str.
54013 Thessaloniki
Tel: +30 (0)2310 378 300
Fax: +30 (0)2310 282 498

Greek State Tourist Office (EOT)
4 Conduit St
London W1S 2DJ
Tel: +44 (0)207 495 9300
Fax: +44 (0)207 287 1369
Website: www.gnto.gr
E-mail: mailto:info@gnto.gr

Ethnikos Organismos Tourismou (EOT)
Tsoha 7
11521 Athens
Tel: +30 (0)210 870 7000
Website: www.gnto.gr
E-mail: mailto:info@gnto.gr

British Embassy
1 Ploutarchou Street
10675 Athens
Tel: +30 (0)210 727 2600, +30 (0)210 727 2720
Website: www.british-embassy.gr
E-mail: information.athens@fco.gov.uk
British consulates: contact the British Embassy or see its website
(above)

Greek Embassy
1a Holland Park
London W11 3TP
Tel: +44 (0)207 229 3850
Fax: +44 (0)207 229 7221
Website: www.greekembassy.org.uk

6 Portugal

Portugal is England's oldest ally, dating back to the Treaty of Alliance in 1373, with the two countries frequently siding together against Portugal's Spanish neighbour. Portugal has a population of around 10 million, most of whom still live in rural areas. The population of the capital Lisbon is just under 700,000, although two million people live in Greater Lisbon. While the Portuguese economy is reasonably strong, it is nevertheless a low-wage economy, with a minimum wage under half that of the United Kingdom, for example. Large numbers of Portuguese have left their home country in search of work abroad, with many going to France, where their numbers easily surpass those of the British in France.

Residence permits and identity cards

Those planning to work in Portugal for longer than three months should apply for a residence permit (*autorizaca de residencia*). Application is made to the local Foreigners' Department of the Ministry of Internal Affairs (*Serviço de Estrangeiros e Fronteiras*). You obtain the application form from British consulates in Portugal, and lodge it with the *junta de freguesia* or local council. Portuguese law stipulates that you must carry your identity card (*bilhete de identidade*) with you at all times.

Finding employment

The government employment service (*Centro do Emprego*) provides advice on job vacancies and training. It comes under the auspices of the *Ministério de Emprego e Seguranca Social*. You can find the contact details of your local office in the telephone directory (*Lista Telefonica*) or the Yellow Pages (*Páginas Amarelas*). You can obtain additional information on jobs and training from the *Instituto do Emprego e Formaçao Profissional* (IEFP), AV Jose Malhoa 11, 1099–018 Lisbon. The website at www.iefp.pt is in Portuguese only.

Employment agencies can be found in the *Páginas Amarelas* (www.paginasamarelas.pt) under *Pessoal Temporário* for temporary appointments and also *Pessoal Recrutamento e Selecca*. Agencies include Manpower (www.manpower.pt), Adecco (www.adecco.pt), and also Ad Capita International Search, Glasford Portugal and Michael Page International. There are relatively few agencies outside Lisbon and Porto. Most national and regional newspapers carry advertisements for job vacancies, including *Publico* (www.publico.pt), *Diário de Notícias* (www.dn.sapo.pt: see under *Classificados* and then *Embrego*), and *Expresso*, which is published weekly (www.expresso.pt). The English-language newspapers are *Anglo-Portuguese News, The News* (in the Algarve), and the weekly publication *The Resident* (www.portugalresident.com) which has editions for both the Algarve and Greater Lisbon. You can also try the British–Portuguese Chamber of Commerce (*Camara de Comercio Luso-Britanica*), which helps its member companies fill vacancies (see below for contact details).

A useful source of information is the *Instituto da Juventude*, whose Lisbon headquarters is at Avenida da Liberdade 194 – R/C, 1250 Lisbon (tel: +35 (0)1 21 352 2694, e-mail: juventude@mail.telepac.pt).

Some Britons are successful in obtaining work through the expatriate community, and it may be worthwhile networking among fellow Britons in Portugal. The contact details for the Portuguese British Association are included below. There is a British Community Council of Lisbon, which seeks to bring English-speaking people together and holds a range of cultural, social and charitable events (see www.bcclisbon.org). There are also branches of the British Council in Lisbon, Porto, and Coimbra (see contact details below). The largest concentrations of Britons in Portugal are in Lisbon or the Algarve.

During the summer months there are jobs to be had in the Algarve, principally along the coast in the hotels, restaurants and bars in the more popular tourist resorts. Accommodation can be quite expensive. There are some opportunities to work on the harvest (see www.fruitfuljobs.com).

There are opportunities to teach English, especially in the major towns. Language schools include the Bristol School Group (www.bristolschool.pt) and the Cambridge School (www.cambridgeschool.pt). You are unlikely to earn more than €1,000 per month, or €15 per hour for individual lessons.

You can obtain information about the Portuguese language (including language courses), and culture from the *Instituo de Cultura e Lingua Portuguesa* at Praça do Principe Real 14–1, 1200 Lisbon.

Banking

There are now nine branches of Barclays in Portugal (www.barclays.pt – click on International Clients for pages in English).

Health

The public health system in Portugal, administered by *Ministério de Saúde*, is more limited than in most other Western European countries. You can find out information by contacting your local *administração regional de Saúde*. You are permitted to choose which doctor to consult, though you must pay for consultations. Prescriptions for some serious illnesses are free. For others, patients either pay 40–70 per cent of the price or have to pay the full price.

The British Embassy keeps a list of doctors and dentists on its website (www.uk-embassy.pt, go to Services – Consular – Useful Information). There is a British Hospital in Lisbon at Rua Saraiva de Carvalho 49, 1269–098 Lisbon (tel.: +35 (0)21 394 3100).

Social security

If you lose your job you should consult your local *Centro do Emprego*. Foreigners can obtain information about their rights from the *Departamento de Relações Internacionais e Convenções da Seguranç Social*, Pua da Junqueira 112, 1300 Lisbon (tel: +35 (0)1 21 362 1633, fax: +35 (0)1 21 363 2725).

Employment rights

Portugal has a legal minimum wage (currently around €500 per month) applicable to all workers aged over 20. Employers must pay those under 20 at least a certain percentage of the legal minimum wage. Salaries are considerably lower than those in the United Kingdom, even allowing for the fact that Portugal is one of the cheapest countries in the European Community to live in. Employees receive two annual bonuses of a month's salary each, paid at Christmas and at the end of June. Portugal operates a maximum working week of 40 hours. Employees receive a statutory minimum of 22 working days' holiday a year, in addition to 12–14 public holidays.

Accommodation

The availability of accommodation in Lisbon and Oporto and also in the Algarve is limited, and by Portuguese standards it is quite expensive. Tenancies are generally for a minimum of six months. There are advertisements for rental properties in most newspapers (see sections headed *alugam-se*). It is definitely worth consulting the *Anglo-Portuguese News* and other English-language publications (see above). As to purchasing property, there are now a number of UK agents with links with local estate agents, which offer assistance in locating properties to buy in Portugal. Details of agents are kept by the Portuguese–UK Chamber of Commerce (contact details below). Reputable Portuguese agents are registered with the *Mediador Autorizado.* The *Anglo-Portuguese News, The News* (published for the Algarve) and *The Resident* (with editions for both the Algarve and Greater Lisbon) carry property advertisements.

Education

Nursery education (*educação pré-escolar*), is available for children aged from three to five. In addition to subsidized pre-schools within the state system, there are various private nurseries. Compulsory school education covers 6 to 15 year olds over three cycles. During the first cycle, spanning four years, pupils have one teacher, often assisted for some lessons. For the second cycle covering the next two years, and the third cycle lasting three years, pupils have specialist teachers for each subject. Having completed their compulsory education pupils can either continue their studies in the regular school system or opt to take vocational or artistic courses.

There are a number of international schools in Portugal, and a few schools that follow the British curriculum (for details see the website of the British–Portuguese Chamber of Commerce: www.bpcc.pt – go to Business Guide then to Living and Working).

Higher education

Institutions of higher education consist of traditional universities, and *institutos politécnicos* which are more vocationally oriented. Students take their degrees over four to six years.

Comparability of qualifications

The contact details for the Portuguese NARIC are:

Direcção-Geral de Ensino Superior, Direcção de Serviços
Pedagógicos,
Divisão de Reconhecimento e Intercâbio, Av. Duque D'Ábvila 137
1069–016 Lisbon
Tel: +35 (0)1 21 312 60 00
Fax: +35 (0)1 21 312 60 01
Website: www.dges.mcies.pt
E-mail: manuela.paiva@dges.mcies.pt

Emergency information

Telephone 115 for fire, police and ambulance services. There is no
charge for these calls.

Useful addresses

Portuguese Embassy
11 Belgrave Square
London
SW1X 8PP
Tel: +44 (0)870 162 0857
Fax: +44 (0)207 245 1287
Website: portugal.embassyhomepage.com
E-mail: mailto:london@portembassy.co.uk

Portuguese Trade and Tourist Office
22–25a Sackville St
London W1X 1DE
Tel: +44 (0)207 494 1441
Fax: +44 (0)207 494 1868
Website: www.portugal.org

British Embassy
Rua de S Bernardo 33
1200 Lisbon
Tel: +35 (0)1 21 392 4000
Fax: +35 (0)1 21 396 6768
Website:www.uk-embassy.pt

The British Council
Rua Luís Fernandes 1–3
1249–062 Lisbon
Tel: +35 (0)1 21 321 45 00
Fax: +35 (0)1 21 347 61 51
Website: www.britishcouncilpt.org
E-mail: lisbon.enquiries@pt.britishcouncil.org

Portuguese British Association
Rua do Breinver, 155/165
4050 Porto
Tel: +35 (0)1 22 205 1485

British–Portuguese Chamber of Commerce,
Rua da Estrela 8
1200–699 Lisbon
E-mail: info@bpcc.pt www.bpcc.pt

Portuguese Chamber of Commerce:
Associaçâo Comercial de Lisboa
Câmera de Comércio e Indústria Portuguesa
Rua das Portas de Santo Antâo 89
1194 Lisbon
Tel: +35 (0)1 21 322 4050
Fax: +35 (0)1 21 322 4051

7 English-speaking Europe (Cyprus and Malta)

Cyprus

Cyprus is the third largest island in the Mediterranean, close to the three continents of Europe, Africa and Asia. The island has been fought over many times in its tumultuous history, with the Greeks, Phoenicians, Romans, Crusaders and Venetians all occupying it at different times. Legend has it that Aphrodite, the mythological goddess of beauty, was born in the warm seas that wash the island's shores. St Paul introduced Christianity to Cyprus as early as 45 AD.

Cyprus is rich in citrus fruits, olive groves and pine-forested mountains. The climate is warm and extremely pleasant, and the island boasts a stunning coastline which combines numerous clean golden beaches with a mountainous backdrop.

The island gained independence in 1960, but in July 1974 was invaded by Turkey. The Turkish army occupied a large part of Cyprus and over 150,000 Greek Cypriots were forcibly expelled. They have yet to return to their homes. The invasion was internationally condemned, and the 'independent state' that was announced in 1983 in the Turkish-controlled part of the island has never been recognized by most other countries.

Today the population of the island is almost 800,000, consisting mostly of Greek Cypriots (85 per cent). The rest of the population is made up of around equal numbers of Turkish Cypriots, who occupy about one-third of the island, and foreigners. Currently only the Greek part of the island is a member of the European

Union, having joined in May 2004. The island's capital is Nicosia. The official language of Cyprus is Greek, though English is widely spoken and Turkish is spoken in the north of the island. The currency is the Cyprus pound.

Immigration and residence documentation

Citizens of EU countries are entitled to enter and stay in Cyprus for up to three months to look for work or to try to start a business, providing they have a full valid 10-year passport. You must request an Alien's Residence Certificate (ARC) from the local police within eight days of arriving. Should you intend to stay to work, study or engage in a business activity for more than three months you must obtain a residence permit by applying to the Civil Registration and Migration Department soon after you arrive. You do not have to wait for your residence permit but can begin work immediately. The permit, which is valid for five years, should be issued to you within six months. You can obtain further information from the Civil Registration and Migration Department (tel: +357 (0)22804401; e-mail: migration@crmd.moi.gov.cy). Citizens from Australia aged 18 to 25 may apply for a one-year holiday working visa for Cyprus.

Turkish Cyprus (population just over 200,000) is not yet part of the European Union. You are generally permitted to stay for only three months, and you will therefore need to leave and return to renew your entitlement if you wish to stay for longer, which foreigners often do by travelling across to Turkey.

Finding employment

Tourism forms the major sector within the Cypriot economy, providing employment during the winter as well as over the summer months, especially in bars and restaurants. Proprietors prefer to take on female staff, although it should be noted that sexual harassment is a common cause of complaint by foreign women carrying out such work. Agriculture also plays a very significant role in the economy, with short-term employment often available for fruit picking (oranges, strawberries and grapes). There are opportunities working for tour operators, and you will find a list of operators on www.tourist-offices.org.uk/Cyprus/uktourops.

There are relatively few opportunities for foreigners in the Turkish-controlled part of the island, except in tourism. Some people obtain work through contacting the Anglo-Cypriot Association.

Those in search of employment in Greek Cyprus should call in at one of the District Labour Offices, which provide advice and assistance to job seekers. In addition to your passport and ARC you will need copies of certificates of your academic and/or professional qualifications. The main offices are:

11 District Labour Offices, Kiniras str.1102 Nicosia
Tel: +357 (0)22303555,
E-mail: dlonic@dl.mlsi.gov.cy

80 Franklin Roosevelt Ave, Limassol
Tel: +357 (0)25804400
E-mail: dlonic@dl.mlsi.gov.cy

Filiou Tsigaridi, 6023 Larnaca
Tel: +357 (0)24304134

Filikis Eterias Str., 8047 Pafos
Tel: +357 (0)26306230

Employment agencies and other assistance for job seekers

The contact details of employment agencies can be obtained from the Cyprus High Commission in London (see below for the address) or the Yellow Pages in Cyprus. The classified sections of two English language newspapers, the *Cyprus Mail* (www.cyprus-mail.com) and the *Cyprus Weekly* (www.cyprusweekly.com.cy), both contain regular selections of job advertisements. You should also visit the website of the Cyprus Chamber of Commerce: www.ccci.org.cy. The website www.cyprusjobs.com generally has a selection of job openings.

Health services

Those with an annual income at or below C£9,000, and families with income at or below C£18,000, receive free health care, as do members of families with four or more children, people suffering from certain chronic diseases, and those in receipt of public welfare payments. Individuals with income up to C£12,000 and families with incomes up to C£22,000 receive subsidized health care. The rest of the population may use the medical facilities provided by the state but are charged the full rate. Accident and emergency provision is free of charge to all, including those visiting the island. Many employers and trade unions arrange private health care schemes for their employees and members.

Social security

EU citizens are entitled to social security cover. Once you start work you will pay contributions to the Cypriot social security system. Employees' contributions amount to 6.3 per cent of income, with the self-employed paying 11.6 per cent. Further details can be obtained from: Department of Social Insurance, 7 Byron Avenue, 1465 Nicosia (tel.: +357 (0)22401632, e-mail: interrel@dsi.mlsi.gov.cy).

Tax

Those who spend more than 183 days per year in the country are considered tax residents and are taxed on their income worldwide. Those who are not residents in Cyprus are only taxed on income earned in Cyprus. The first C£10,000 of income is free of tax, after which income is taxed at 20 per cent on the next C£5,000, 25 per cent on a further C£5,000 and thereafter at 30 per cent.

Employment issues

There is no national minimum wage in Cyprus, thought Cypriot law does stipulate a minimum wage (currently around €600 per month) for a number of occupations, namely clerical workers, sales staff, auxiliary health care employees and auxiliary staff in schools, nursery schools and crèches. In addition there are collective agreements in several industries which provide for minimum terms and conditions for workers. Average earnings are significantly lower than elsewhere in the European Union.

Working time and leave

Employees in Cyprus work an average of around 38 hours per week and may not work for more than 48 hours in a week. They are entitled to a minimum of three weeks' paid leave a year, though they must first have worked for 13 weeks in the holiday year. Most employees, however, receive four weeks' holiday, plus an additional 15 days by way of public holidays.

Accommodation

Both rental property and property for sale are dealt with by estate agents. Contact details of agents can be obtained from the Cyprus Real Estate Agents Association, PO Box 1455, Lefkosia (tel: +357) 0449500) or from the Cyprus Government Tourist Office. Accommodation is in good supply, both apartments and houses. Reasonable flats cost from C €500 per month to rent. Foreigners intending to purchase a property in Cyprus are required to obtain a permit. Applications are made to the local district office.

Education

There are both public and private facilities for pre-school education for children from the age of three. A fee is payable for both. Compulsory free education at primary school (*Dimotiko Scholeio*) runs from the age of five. At 11 children then attend compulsory secondary school (*Gymnasio*) until the age of 15. Those children in difficulties in the last year of primary school may be required to repeat the year. During their last year at the *Gymnasio* pupils take compulsory examinations (*telikes exetaseis*).

After the *Gymnasio* students can remain at school for a second non-compulsory stage of secondary education to age 18 in either the *Eniaio Lykeio* or the more academic *Lykeio Epilogis Mathimaton.* Both prepare pupils for the *apolytirio,* the entrance examinations for third-level education. A third alternative is the more vocational *Techniki Scholi.*

Higher education

You will find links to most of the third-level educational establishments on the website for the University of Cyprus: www.ucy.ac.cy. Institutes of higher education fall into three categories: the *Panepistimio* or university providing four-year courses, the public-sector *Dimosies Scholes Tritovathmias Ekpaidefsis* offering three-year courses, and the private-sector *Idiotikes Scholes Tritovathmias Ekpaidefsis,* which has a range of courses of different duration.

Comparability of qualifications

Contact details for the Cypriot NARIC are:

Cyprus Council for the Recognition of Higher Education Qualifications (KYSATS)
Ministry of Education and Culture
Thoukididou and Kimonos Corner
CY 1434 Nicosia
Tel: +357 (0)22 800666; Fax: +357(0)22 305116
E-mail: kysats@cytanet.com.cy
Website: www.moec.gov.cy/

Emergency information

Call 112 for fire, police and ambulance services. These calls are free.

Useful addresses and web sites

Cyprus High Commission,
93 Park St,
London W1K 7ET
Tel: +44 (0)870 005 6711
Fax: +44 (0)207 491 0691

British High Commission,
Alexander Pallis Street, PO Box 21978
1587+357 (0)22 861100
E-mail: infobhc@cylink.com.cy

www.visitcyprus.org.cy, www.cyprusairways.com,
www.yourcyprus.com, europa.eu.int/comm/enlargement/
cyprus/index.htm

Malta

Situated in the middle of the Mediterranean, the small island of
Malta has a rich history, with its people originating from a melting
pot of different cultures. Its capital city is Valletta, its official
languages are Maltese and English, and its currency is the lira,
often referred to as the Maltese pound. The island enjoys a warm
climate with extremely mild winters. Its population of around
380,000 is swollen by the steady flow of tourists visiting the island,
who generally receive a friendly welcome. Malta's smaller sister
island of Gozo is considered more of a backwater, and is much
quieter and more rustic than Malta. A regular ferry service
connects the two islands.

Following Malta's entry into the European Union in May 2004,
EU nationals might expect to be entitled to enter Malta to work or
to study, or to set up a business. However, Malta negotiated a
seven-year period until 2011 during which it may unilaterally
impose restrictions on the numbers entering, should the influx of
EU workers put an undue strain on local labour markets.

Furthermore, those intending to work are required to have an employment licence before travelling to Malta. The licence should be obtained by the employer. The employer must demonstrate to the Maltese authorities that it has made sufficient efforts to recruit a Maltese citizen for the position. Further information can be obtained from the Department for Citizenship and Expatriate Affairs, 3 Castille Place, Valletta.

Non-EU citizens are not permitted to work in Malta at all, or to carry out business there, though Australian citizens under 30 are permitted to work on the island for 12 months under the umbrella of the Working Holiday Visa Program. If non-EU nationals wish to take up permanent residence they must provide evidence of capital in excess of LM150,000 or an annual income of LM10,000.Those wishing simply to visit or study in Malta who are citizens of a British Commonwealth country, the United States, Japan or of course the European Union, will not normally require a visa.

Working

The website of the Department of Citizenship and Expatriates at www.etc.gov.mt has useful information for those seeking to work in Malta, including job vacancies. The majority of non-Maltese employed on the island work in the tourist industry. There is also a substantial demand for teachers of English as a foreign language – there are nearly 60 language schools on the island. Some occupations, such as law, make fluency in Maltese a condition of entry and practice. The prospects of obtaining a job and a licence are highest for those working in computers, technology, sales or translation work. The salaries in these sectors, while high for Malta (up to around €1,000 per month), remain low compared with the rest of the European Union. There is also a current shortage of nurses on Malta (for information contact Malta Nurses Association: PO Box 63, Hamrun, Malta).

Other sectors that tend to have vacancies include the construction industry, the catering and the restaurant trade; security officers, lorry drivers and other drivers, clerks, beauticians and hairdressers can usually find employment. Over a quarter of the workforce on Malta are employed directly in the tourist industry.

The employment service

Job seekers should register with the Employment and Training Corporation at Hal Far. In addition, or alternatively, you can consult the website of the Maltese State Employment Service: www.etc.gov.mt. This includes an online vacancy database. Jobs can be searched for by occupation and locality.

Other means of finding vacancies

The main newspapers are worth consulting: the *Times of Malta* (www.timesofmalta.com) and the *Independent* (www.independent. com.mt). There are a number of recruitment agencies to contact, including Misco, 3rd Floor Regency House, Republic Street, Valletta VLT04 (tel: +356 (0)21 22 03 03) and Outlook, Mikelang Refalo Avenue, Balzan BZN 07 (tel: +356(0) 2144 1604, e-mail: info@outlook.coop, website: www.outlook.coop).

The following websites contain advertisements for job vacancies and/or useful information for job seekers: www.vacancycentre.com, www.people.com.mt, www.etc.org.mt, www.il-monti.com and www.maltalinks/com.

The Chamber of Commerce is an invaluable source of information about potential employers. The contact details are: Chamber of Commerce, Exchange Buildings, Republic Street, Valletta VLT05 (tel: +356 (0)21 233 873, e-mail: admin@chamber.org.mt, website: www.chamber.org.mt).

In Malta many job vacancies are filled by word of mouth. Accordingly it pays to network. If you are determined to work in Malta it would be worthwhile considering an initial trip as a visitor.

Working conditions

Malta has a national minimum wage, which is currently around LM55 per week (plus bonuses), for all workers over 18. Workers receive annual pay increases linked to the cost of living. The normal working week in Malta is 40 hours, and employees are entitled to 25 days' paid annual leave in addition to the 13 days of public holidays.

The government website www.gov.mt includes links to information about a wide range of issues, ranging from job vacancies (including employment opportunities for those with a disability) to employment rights generally and training options. There is also a facility to post your CV online.

Expatriates

A British Residents Association with members from all nationalities is active in Malta and Gozo, and holds various social events. There is the Anglican Cathedral of St Paul's in Valletta and an Anglican church in Sliema, the Church of the Holy Trinity. There is a Church of Scotland congregation and also a Methodist congregation, which both meet at St Andrews (Scots) Church, South Street, Valletta, as well as many Catholic churches with masses in English.

Health care and social security

There is a free national health service on Malta financed by Maltese taxpayers. The service is free at the point of delivery, and accordingly you are not required to pay first and then seek reimbursement. Patients do have to pay for medicines, although those on low incomes are entitled to receive these free of charge, as are those who have certain chronic illnesses.

If you lose your job, you should contact the Employment and Training Corporation (www.etc.gov.mt) or visit the Employment Services Division, Hal Far (tel: +356 (0)21 654 940). Your employer should provide you with a Termination of Employment certificate. The Employment and Training Corporation is also responsible has a number of schemes to help the unemployed and school leavers to find work, including assistance with training. For the moment, however, these schemes will not be of assistance to many EU citizens given the restrictions that will apply until the year 2011.

Taxation

You must complete an annual self-assessment tax return. This must be filed and payment made by the 15 June each year. Permanent residents (generally those who stay in Malta for more than 183 days in a year) are taxed on their worldwide income. They receive a personal allowance of LM3,000 (LM4,300 for those who are married). The next LM1,000 is taxed at 15 per cent, with additional income being taxed at higher rates, up to a top rate of 35 per cent on income of over LM6,750. Non-residents have a tax-free allowance of only LM300 and pay the top rate of 35 per cent on all income over LM3,300. You can obtain further details form the website www.ird.gov.mt. Income from employment is taxed at source by deductions made by the employer.

Accommodation

Malta has a plentiful supply of short-term rental accommodation. A deposit of one month's rent is generally payable by way of guarantee. This is repayable when you leave. Estate agents charge a commission of one month's rent, which is split equally between the landlord and tenant. There are some restrictions on foreigners purchasing property in Malta: they are limited to owning one property only, and they are forbidden from buying apartments costing under LM30,000 and houses less than LM50,000. Prospective purchasers who are not permanent residents must apply to the Ministry of Finance for permission to buy. You can obtain lists of property for rental or for sale from the Association of Malta Estate Agents. Estate agency websites include www.propertylinemalta.com and www.franksalt.com.mt.

Education

The standard of education in Malta, including in the public education system, is considered to be high. Children are educated in English in accordance with a curriculum and examination system that is very similar to that in the United Kingdom. There are several private schools, including boarding schools. A considerable number of people on the island speak Italian, though French and German are also studied in schools. There are also a number of international schools in Malta, some closely following the UK curriculum and others offering the more European baccalaureate. Information can be obtained from the European Council for International Schools.

A wide range of information, including lists of primary and secondary state, church and independent schools and links to many of the schools' websites, can be obtained from the government's Department of Education website at www.education.gov.mt.

Pre-school

Parents can send children to state or private kindergarten from the age of three. Most of the primary state schools also provide pre-primary education. At primary level there are state, church and some private fee-paying schools. In state schools primary education is from the age of five, and divided into two cycles each lasting three years. Church schools do not make this division.

State secondary schools consist of Junior Lyceum schools and area secondary schools. The former admit about half the secondary school population and are selective, with pupils only admitted after taking an entrance examination.

At the end of their secondary education school leavers are issued with a leaving certificate. Of greater importance for admission to upper secondary education and for job applications is the Secondary Education Certificate (SEC), which is issued by the education board MATSEC. The upper-secondary level education consists of two years and can be studied at University Junior College (attached to the University of Malta), in the sixth form of state schools, or in church and private schools. Information about the College is at www.jc.um.edu.mt.

Third-level education

Information concerning the University of Malta can be found on its website at www.um.edu.mt/faculties.html. Students are required to obtain the MATSEC Certificate as a condition of entry (www.jc.um.edu.mt). Again the language of instruction is English. There are almost 7,000 students studying a wide range of disciplines.

Comparability of qualifications

Contact details for the Maltese NARIC are:

Malta NARIC,
Ministry of Education
Room No 328, Great Siege Road
Floriana CMR 02, Malta
Tel: +356 (0)21 240 419
Fax: +356 (0)21 239 842
E-mail: qric.malta@gov.mt
Website: www.education.gov.mt/

Emergency information

Telephone 112 for fire, police and ambulance services. These calls are free.

Useful addresses

Maltese High Commission in the United Kingdom
36–38 Piccadilly
London W1V 0PP
Tel: +44 (0)20 729 24800
Fax: +44 (0)20 773 41831
E-mail: maltahighcommission.London@gov.mt
Website: www.malta.embassyhomepage.com/index.htm

British High Commission in Malta
P.O. Box 506, 7 St Anne Street
Floriana, Valletta
Tel: +365 (0)2331 3487

Malta Tourism Authority
Auberge d'Italie, Merchants Street
Valletta CMR 02
Tel: +356 (0)2291 5000
Website: www.mta.com.mt

The following websites are worth a visit: www.aboutmalta.com,
www.gov.mt, www.visitmalta.com and www.maltacom.com

8 The United States

The two most popular states with the British are definitely Florida and California. Accordingly this chapter deals primarily with those seeking employment in those two states, though much of the information applies throughout the United States.

Most foreigners are not allowed to remain in the United States for more than three months, unless they have a residence permit (the 'green card') or a visa. Visitors must also be in possession of a passport that will remain valid for at least six months after the end of their trip to the United States.

The United States welcomes over 800,000 lawful immigrants each year, with Florida and California being two of the most popular destinations for new arrivals. Over half of these immigrants rely on a marriage or family connection. The balance includes about 140,000 employment-based immigrants, around 120,000 refugees, and 55,000 winners of the diversity lottery (see below). In addition there is a sizeable number of illegal immigrants. Many of these have crossed over from Mexico or Canada, but a larger number consist of those who have legitimately entered the United States on student, tourist or business visas but have not returned to their home country.

The procedure for migrating to the United States is long and bureaucratic. It was administered by the Immigration and Naturalization Service (INS), but this is now known as the Bureau of Citizenship and Immigration Services (BCIS) and comes under the auspices of the Office of Homeland Security. While you will find more detailed information in books specializing on this subject, and on various internet sites, those intent on permanent immigration to the United States should seriously consider consulting an experienced immigration attorney who will be able to provide you with

BUNAC's
Working Adventures Worldwide

BUNAC, the British Universities North America Club, is a leading provider of work and volunteer opportunities around the world for students and other young people. Taking part in a BUNAC programme offers you an exciting opportunity to spend time living and working in a new country. It also gives you the chance to meet a whole new circle of friends from all over the world, be truly independent and gain some amazing life skills and experience. BUNAC's UK office provides comprehensive help, advice and information throughout the course of the application procedure. Support services are available overseas from each of BUNAC's partner organisations.

Flexible year-long programmes

If you're looking to spend up to a full year living and working overseas, *Work Canada, Work Australia, Work New Zealand* and *Work South Africa* are ideal working holiday destinations. On these programmes, participants can take virtually any type of work, anywhere in the country although most choose to finance the trip by taking casual employment in the summer hospitality or tourism industry. There is also however the option to work in one of the popular ski resorts in Canada or on New Zealand's South island.

Application Forms are available to download from the BUNAC website. Please note there is a limited number of places available on *Work Canada* so early application is strongly advised.

Volunteering placements

Open year-round, BUNAC's volunteer programmes offer the more adventurous or experienced traveller a unique opportunity to contribute to a worthwhile cause, often within a local community, while exploring a completely new way of life. To apply to *Volunteer Ghana, Volunteer South Africa, Volunteer Peru, Volunteer Costa Rica* or *Volunteer Cambodia*, you will need to be flexible, confident and able to throw yourself 100% into your placement; Spanish speaking skills are also required for Peru and Costa Rica.

Working as a volunteer allows participants to fully integrate into a community and have a truly satisfying work abroad experience. Placements last from as little as eight weeks to as long as a year.

Summer camp opportunities

Summer Camp USA and *KAMP USA* offer eligible applicants the chance to spend a fun and rewarding summer working on a US children's camp. On *KAMP USA*, full-time students are placed in a support role on camp while students and non-students aged 18/19-35, with experience of working with children, can work as camp counsellors. Benefits of these programmes include low upfront costs, a competitive in-hand salary and free food and accommodation for the time you are on camp. Recruitment starts in November.

Summer work and travel

An alternative way for full-time UK university level students to enjoy a warm American summer is by taking part in *Work America*. On this programme, you can take almost any sort of paid work in the USA and explore the country – plus Canada and Mexico – while you're there. Application forms are available from the BUNAC website from November. Participants usually fly to the US in June/early July and return in September/early October in time for the start of the new academic year.

For further information on BUNAC's full range of programmes or to check eligibility, contact:

BUNAC
16 Bowling Green Lane
London
EC1R 0QH
Tel: (020) 7251 3472
E-mail: enquiries@bunac.org.uk
Website: www.bunac.org

preliminary advice on the best route to take for a fixed fee of around US $300. You should also consider instructing an attorney to file the papers on your behalf, as it is very easy for those unfamiliar with the system to make an unnecessary error that results in the application being refused or delayed. The lawyer's services can be expensive, depending on the complexities involved in your application and the time taken to prepare it.

Those entering the United States are classified as either immigrants (those wishing to settle permanently in the United States) or non-immigrants (temporary residents).

Immigrants

Immigrants are entitled to work permanently in the United States, and qualify for US citizenship after five years. The categories of immigrants include:

- the spouse, child, parent, widow or widower of a US citizen;

- other family members of US citizens;

- foreigners with outstanding abilities or skills, or investors with generally at least US $1 million capital and who will be employing 10 or more US persons;

- religious workers;

- employees of the United States abroad;

- diversity lottery immigrants (see below);

- refugees from persecution.

Immediate relatives

The spouse, child, parent, widow or widower of a US citizen is entitled, as of right, to an immigrant visa. There is no limit on the number of those entitled to a visa on this ground.

Family-based immigration

Those entitled to apply are the unmarried son or daughter over 21 of a US citizen, the spouse or unmarried son or daughter of a lawful permanent resident, the brother or sister of a US citizen over 21, and the married son or daughter of a US citizen. There is an annual quota for visas in this category (of around 200,000), and applicants often have to wait several years before they are successful.

Employment-based immigration (EB)

Usually successful applicants must have a specific offer of employment from an employer based in the United States. There is an annual quota, and five sub-categories that take up the quota in order of preference, with most applicants falling into the first three categories. Priority is firstly given to those with exceptional ability in the sciences, education, the arts or sport, outstanding professors and researchers, and some multinational executives and managers. In the second category are professionals with advanced degrees and workers with exceptional ability in the sciences, arts or business. The third category covers professionals, skilled and unskilled workers. Employers sponsoring applicants in the second and third category must satisfy the Department of Labor that the position cannot be filled by a US worker. The Labor Certification process is notoriously slow.

The diversity/green card lottery

Every year the United States makes available 55,000 'diversity' visas to natives of foreign countries from which immigration in the previous five years was less than 50,000 people (Section 131 of the Immigration Act 1990). Applicants from such countries must have been educated to at least high school level, or have worked for at least two of the previous five years in an occupation that requires two years or more of training or experience. The United Kingdom is not a low admission country, but Ireland is (and this includes Northern Ireland). You do not have to be resident in your native country at the time of application, and accordingly UK residents who were born in Ireland or Northern Ireland may apply. The spouse of a native of a 'low-admission' country is also entitled to apply. Those eligible to enter the lottery may do so in addition to submitting any visa application, and may make repeat applications in subsequent years.

Dates for submitting lottery applications change, and you should check with the Department of State, which is responsible for administering the lottery, not the BCIS. The website is www.travel.state.gov. No fee is charged, and there is no application form. Those wishing to enter the diversity lottery must do so by e-mail, providing basic personal details and photographs of themselves, their spouse and any children under 18 who will accompany them to the United States if they are successful.

Non-immigrants

Those with a non-immigrant visa are permitted to enter and to stay in the United States for a limited period of time, and for limited purposes. No separate work permit is required: those permitted to work will have this recorded on their visa. The visa categories are: Government officials (A), Visitor (B-1, B-2),Transit (C), Crew (D), Treaty trader or investor (E-1, E-2), Academic student (F), International organization representative (G), Speciality occupation workers (H-1B, these include in particular nurses, and those providing services that are in short supply in the United States), Temporary workers (H-2B), Foreign press (I), Student/teacher exchange (J), Fiancée/fiancé (K), Intracompany transfers (L-1), Non-academic student (M), Parent/child/sibling of alien granted special immigrant status (N), Aliens of extraordinary ability (O), Athletes/entertainers (P); Cultural exchange (Q); Religious workers (R); Professional – Canadian/Mexican NAFTA (TN). Up-to-date information about visas can be obtained from and via the website of the US Embassy in London: www.usembassy.org.uk.

When entering or re-entering the United States those in possession of a non-immigrant visa should carry proof of their entitlement with them (such as possession of sufficient funds to support themselves, a return ticket and evidence of the purpose of their trip), as immigration officials are not obliged to accept the visa at face value but may investigate whether its holder is lawfully qualified to enter the United States. Those entering the United States without a visa, or on a business or tourist visa, are not permitted to engage in any form of paid or unpaid employment, though many thousands of visitors breach this rule. The US immigration officials can ask extremely searching questions and often subject entrants to rigorous searches. You could be refused entry if they find any suggestion that you have arranged or will be looking for illegal work. If you have a full-time job that you will be returning to in the United Kingdom, or an offer of a place in a further education establishment, it will ease your passage through immigration if you have some evidence of this with you. Note that all children entering the United States must have their own passport, and cannot be included on a parent's passport.

It can take up to two months for a visa application to be processed, although in many cases applicants receive their visas within a month of lodging their application. It is possible to extend a tourist visa, providing you can demonstrate an acceptable reason for your request, and you have the means to continue to support yourself without working.

The B visas

Unless they are natives of a country covered by the visa waiver scheme (see below), travellers to the United States on holiday must apply for a B-2 visa. The application form can be downloaded from www.travel.state.gov. Go to DS-156.pdf. Business travellers not covered by the visa waiver scheme should apply for a B-1 visa.

Visa waivers

Nationals of certain countries can visit the United States under a visa waiver scheme. The countries covered include the United Kingdom, Ireland, Australia, New Zealand, all the Scandinavian countries, the Netherlands, most other EU countries and Japan. You must be in possession of a valid passport, and a return or onward non-transferable ticket, though this latter provision does not apply if you arrive by land from Canada or Mexico. The trip must be for business or pleasure, and is limited to 90 days. Note that all those wishing to enter under the visa waiver scheme must have a machine-readable passport. The old blue UK passports are insufficient, and holders should obtain a visa or a new UK passport.

The E2 visa

The E2 visa enables individuals who make an investment in a US-based business, or who start up their own business in the United States, to stay in the country. While the individual will normally be granted a stay of two years, this can be extended, and in practice investors remain for the whole of the period during which their investment continues. The spouse and children under 21 of such investors also have the right to stay in the United States and attend school. Furthermore, the investor's spouse is also permitted to work, though he or she must apply for a work authorization document from the local branch of the USCIS (United States Citizen and Immigration Service). Children are not entitled to work and can no longer rely on their parent's entitlement once they reach 21, and may therefore have to leave the United States. Any type of business is permitted. While you can apply direct to the immigration authorities, it is advisable to apply through your local US Embassy or consulate. The official responsible often has a considerable degree of discretion, and you should contact him or her before lodging your application. Ideally you should try to speak to the person concerned for an informal discussion.

An applicant must make a 'substantial investment' in the United States. You will see frequent mention of a figure of US $100,000. This is only a guideline: US law has not fixed any minimum level. Whether an investment is sufficient to be determined as 'substantial' depends on the particular circumstances, and it could be much less than this guideline. The investment must be a substantial part of the particular business in question. In many sectors, especially in the service industry, it is possible to start a new business with far less than US $100,000, perhaps even well under half that amount. What the authorities are looking for is for the investor to bring a benefit to the local economy, in particular in terms of employment of US workers. A business employing two or three people (in addition to the investor and his or her family) will frequently be sufficient. So too might be a business supported with a well-argued business plan that does not employ anyone initially, but has good prospects of doing so within the first year, or even of engaging sub-contractors. With some businesses – for example a restaurant – it is easy to show that the business will need the labour of persons other than the investor and his or her immediate family. In some cases the authorities will allow investors a longer period for the envisaged employment of US citizens, though the limit is five years.

If you are purchasing a business, it is usual to place the purchase price in an 'escrow account', with payment to the vendor to be conditional upon the approval of the purchaser's E2 visa application. You are not required to make your investment before you receive confirmation that you have been granted an E2 visa, but you must be able to demonstrate that you have the funds available.

The investor must be able to show that he or she has sufficient control over the business to be able to influence its development. In practice this means at least 50 per cent ownership. Thus two foreigners could together purchase a business, with each having a 50 per cent ownership, and both be able to apply for E2 visas.

The most commonly used working visas (H, L, E)

The H-1B Speciality occupation workers visa

This is for speciality occupation workers. It essentially covers professionals such as accountants, lawyers, teachers and software specialists. A prospective employer will need to show that:

■ the applicant has the equivalent of at least a bachelor's degree;

■ the job is one that ordinarily requires the degree that the prospective employee has;

■ the employer will pay the applicant at least the prevailing salary for that position.

The visa is initially valid for up to three years, and can be extended for a further three years. Spouses and children are granted H-4 visas but are not permitted to work.

The H-1C Registered nurse visa

The United States grants a number of visas annually to those coming to provide nursing care in sectors in which there is a shortage.

The H-2 Temporary worker visa

This enables employers to hire skilled or semi-skilled foreigners in posts for which the employer has a temporary need that cannot be met by appointing a US worker. The employer must first go through the Department of Labor to obtain a grant of a temporary labor certificate, once it has determined that there are no US workers that can fill the post. The visa is initially valid for 12 months. It can be extended for two further 12-month periods. Dependants are given an H-4 visa and may not work.

The L-1 Intracompany transferee visa

This is a frequently used category, and covers executives, managers and those with specialized knowledge who are transferred to the United States within an international organization. To constitute an international organization, the parent company must have a branch office, subsidiary company or affiliate company in the United States. The subsidiary or affiliate company must be at least 50 per cent owned by the foreign parent company. Accordingly, it is possible for those owning a foreign company to transfer themselves to the United States by setting up a branch office, or establishing a subsidiary or an affiliate in the United States. L2 visas are given to family members, who are not authorized to work.

The E-1 Treaty traders and investors visa

This covers investors and traders who wish to carry on their trade or business in the United States. The trade must be between the United States and the country of which the holder is a national, and the country must be one with which the United States has a treaty.

The North American Free Trade Agreement (TN)

This agreement provides additional non-immigrant visa cate-gories (TN) for citizens of Canada and Mexico. For the most part this covers only professional workers. Canadians may also apply for L-1 and H-1 at land border ports of entry and designated airports. You will need documentary evidence to prove eligibility. Entrants can work in the United States for up to one year, but can apply to renew annually. The arrangements are intended to enable Canadians to have their applications for visas processed quickly and with the minimum amount of paperwork. The speed at which applications are decided varies according to the border post. Once in the United States TN status immigrants can apply for H, L or E status.

The J-1 (Teacher/student exchange) and Q-1 (Cultural exchange) visas

Each year a substantial number of people enter the United States on J-1 visas that are granted to enable them to take part in one of a number of government approved schemes under the Exchange Visitor Programme, such as those run by Camp America. Holders are entitled to undertake paid employment, and apply for a social security number. The Q visa is another means of obtaining employment in the United States. This is the Cultural exchange visa. Holders are authorized to work in the United States for up to 15 months in employment in which they share the history, traditions and culture of their own country. Application for this visa is made by the prospective employer, who must obtain approval from the Immigration and Naturalization Service. These visas are usually granted to people taken on to work in summer schools, amusement parks and restaurants in which knowledge of a foreign country is pertinent.

The F-1 (Student) visa

Those permitted to stay in the United States on an F-1 student visa are entitled to work up to 20 hours per week.

Those working in the United States illegally

In addition to the large number of British people working legally in the United States, it is believed that there are tens of thousands working unlawfully throughout the United States, with the highest concentration in California, especially in San Francisco and Los Angeles. The immigration authorities endeavour to impose severe restrictions limiting the ability of illegal immigrants to obtain work. All US employers are required by law to inspect the identification papers of all job applicants to ensure that they are entitled to work in the United States, and can be fined for employing those not authorized. Notwithstanding this there are large numbers of foreigners employed illegally, especially at harvest time in the agricultural sector and during the high season in the tourist industry.

Employment

Career One Stop (www.careeronestop.org)

This concept is designed for job seekers, students, employers and others associated with the employment market, and has links to www.CareerInfoNet.org and to America's Job Bank, www.ajb.com. Tools include precedents to assist in writing CVs and correspondence with prospective employers; programmes to enable you to assess your own skills and training requirements, to improve your career prospects or change career; a notification service that alerts you to the posting of job offers corresponding to your skills; details of benefits for which you might be eligible; and information as to current salary levels for particular job sectors.

Florida has one of the best job creation programmes in the United States. For details visit the official website www.myflorida.com. Employ Florida Marketplace www.employflorida.com provides a job search facility, information on education and training and career assistance. This is said to be one of the most sophisticated sites, and helps to match employers and employees.

You can also make contact with recruitment agencies by sending them a CV and covering letter requesting an appointment. Scan the classified ads in main newspapers. These include the local British press, notably the *Union Jack*, America's national monthly newspaper for Britons, and in Florida the local Canadian press. Also visit the various expatriate websites. When sending unsolicited letters and CVs to companies do not use A4 size paper but rather the standard US size which is 8.5 in x 11 in.

While there is no particular time that employers recruit, September and January are considered to be the best times to search for a new job. Consider using voice mail, and prepare a half-minute slot selling yourself. Foreign qualifications will not mean much to a US employer, so you should have your qualifications assessed, for example by Education International, 29 Denton Road, Wellesley, MA 02181.

Note that large British companies with a substantial presence in Florida and California employ local US workers, and do not recruit from among British citizens in search of work in Florida or California or seeking to move there. There are, however, many Britons (and in Florida, Canadians) employed in businesses specializing in supplying a service to the British and Canadian English communities in Florida and California, especially in the main population centres. Many expatriates find employment opportunities by networking among fellow expatriates.

An ability to speak Spanish is obviously an advantage given the number of Florida and California residents of Hispanic origin, many of whom have only a poor command of English. There is also a very sizeable Canadian population (especially retired people who spend several months in Florida to avoid the bitter Canadian winter). Many of those from Quebec have only a limited knowledge of English, and accordingly there are openings for those with a high level of French in the various businesses run by and for French Canadians.

Teaching

For obvious reasons this is a huge employment sector. For a whole range of details about teaching, including jobs, see www.teachinflorida.com and www.teachcalifornia.org.

Nursing

Again this is a sector employing large numbers of people in Florida and California, and there are frequently shortages and opportunities for foreigners. The United States grants temporary H-1C visas to a number of foreigners each year. You should begin by contacting the Commission on Graduates of Foreign Nursing

Schools and the International Commission on Healthcare Professionals (CGFNS/ICHP), 3600 Market Street, Suite 400, Philadelphia, PA 19104–2651 (tel: +10 (215) 349–8767, e-mail: info@cgfns.org). Take a look at its website at: www.cgfns.org.

Tourism

Not surprisingly tourism is a major industry in both states, and there is a huge demand for jobs in this sector. For the most part they are relatively poorly paid.

Jobs with the state government

Take a look at the website www.peoplefirst.myflorida.com/l ogon.htm where you will find details of employment in the public sector in Florida. For similar positions in California see the website of the California State Board, www.spb.ca.gov.

Job search websites

These include www.getajob.com, www.jobbankusa.com, www. floridajobs.org, www.caljobs.ca.gov, www.californiajobs.com and www.cajobs.com.

Publications

Among those that could be useful are *How to Obtain a Job in the USA*, available from www.immigrationagency.com (cost approx $60) and *How to Get a Job in America* by Roger Jones (2005).

Summer jobs and opportunities for students

One of the main organizers of the student work and travel programmes to the United States is the British Universities North America Club (BUNAC) at 16 Bowling Green Lane,

London EC1R OQH (tel: +44 (0)207 251 3472, website: www.bunac.org.uk). BUNAC is authorized to issue J-1 visas. It organizes work for anyone over 18 in the thousands of summer camps that take place each year in the US, either as camp counsellors in charge of the children, or as part of the teams responsible for providing meals and maintaining the camps. At the end of the camp participants normally have several weeks in which they may remain in the United States before returning home. In addition BUNAC operates a scheme called the 'Work America Programme' under which those in full-time university education can apply for any summer jobs in the United States. BUNAC organizes flights and insurance and is able to make loans to participants. It also produces a Job Directory to assist participants in finding employment. It is also worth consulting *Summer Jobs in the USA* published by Peterson's Guides.

There are a number of other organizations that have similar programmes, including IST Plus Ltd (see www.istplus.com) and Camp America (37A, Queen's Gate, London SW7 5HR (tel: +44 (0)207 581 7333, website: www.campamerica.co.uk).

In Florida there is a huge demand for labour to gather in the citrus crops. The same is true of the tourist industry during the high season, both in the coastal resorts and in America's numerous theme parks, such as those operated by Universal Studios in Orlando, Florida and Hollywood, California (for details, see www.universalstudios.com). Pay in the summer resorts is generally very low, often well under US $3 an hour. On the other hand food and accommodation are often provided free of charge, and it is possible to earn a considerable amount in tips. The best time to arrive is when American students are beginning to leave (in the latter half of August), or before they arrive (that is, in April or May).

A considerable number of British students have had some success in working as door-to-door sales people. Americans tend to be rather more receptive than Europeans to this practice, and in many cases are especially friendly towards Anglo-Saxons from the other side of the Atlantic seeking to fund a stay in the United States. At least one US business recruits students from the United Kingdom (see www.southwestern.com). Another field in which Britons are especially welcome is the teaching of soccer, a sport that is rapidly gaining popularity in the United States (see for example the website www.gapyear.com and also www.soccer-academy.com).

There are numerous opportunities in nursing and childcare, where there are serious shortages of suitable candidates. Qualified child carers, and those under 26 with recent experience in some form of childcare and a clean driving licence, are in an excellent position to obtain a post, and should consult the websites www.aupairamerica.co.uk and www.aupair-agency.com.

There is a wide range of opportunities to carry out voluntary work in the United States, including with BUNAC. An internet search should reveal many different organizations offering a host of different activities.

One way in which students often travel around the United States at low cost is by delivering cars across America. Often the owners want to use their vehicle at their holiday destination some distance from their home, but wish to fly rather than drive. There are large number of Canadian snowbirds (retired Canadians who spend each bitter Canadian winter in the Florida sun) who fall into this category. There are several companies that specialize in making the necessary arrangements, including Auto Driveaway Company (see www.autodriveaway.com).

Starting and running a business in the United States

Starting a business in the United States is probably one of the easiest routes to residency. There are thousands of small British-run businesses in the United States (for a list of those in Florida see the Florida Association of British Business (FABB), website: www.BritishFlorida.com). An E-2 Treaty investor visa (see above) is valid for up to five years. With the substantial increase in UK house prices over the past decade, the ability to invest US$100,000 (or possibly substantial less: see above) is well within the reach of many UK homeowners.

There are various agencies that provide help and assistance in establishing a business. Prior to arriving in the United States you should take a look at the website of the British–American Business Council at www.babc.org. The Council has 30 chapters across the United States including three in California (San Francisco, Los Angeles and Orange County) and two in Florida (Tampa and Orlando). The chapters frequently organize seminars, conferences, discussions and workshops, and are a vital source of information and contacts for those carrying out business in the United States.

You should also contact the local US Chamber of Commerce – a full list of those in Florida can be found at www.sunnybrits.com (go to Resources) – and your local Small Business Administration Center. Take a look at Florida Trend's *Florida Small Business* magazine (available in public libraries). Ask what other help and assistance is available. In relation to exporting goods information is available from the Division of International Trade at Enterprise Florida (see www.eflorida.com, tel: +10 (305) 569 2650).

Business structures

There are four main structures for running a business in the United States:

■ **Sole trader/proprietor**: this is simple both to set up and to close down. A sole trader is personally liable for the business's debts and losses, though in some states, such as Florida, the law protects the business proprietor's home from creditors. Profits are taxed at the individual's federal rate of tax.

■ **In partnership**, where two or more people put capital into the business and share its liabilities. Partnerships are also easy to establish, although it is preferable to have a written partnership agreement drawn up setting out the terms clearly. It is not so easy to dissolve a partnership. The income from the business is declared on each partner's individual tax return. Again, partners remain personally liable. One option is to form a limited partnership, with limited liability. Limited partnerships must be registered at the Division of Corporations at the state's Department of State. A fee is payable for the appointment of a registered agent (US $35 in Florida) and there is also a filing fee. The latter varies from state to state. In Florida it starts at US $52.50 and can rise to US $1,750.

■ **A limited liability company (LLC).** As in the United Kingdom, if the business should fail, the owners' liabilities are limited to the value of their shares in the company. It is a common requirement, however, for a company's bank, or the landlord of the business premises, to insist on personal guarantees from directors or the major shareholders. LCCs must be registered with the Division of Corporations at the Department of State, and pay a filing fee for a new company (US $125 in Florida). Thereafter a small yearly payment is required. You can choose whether the LLC is taxed as a partnership or as a corporation.

■ **A corporation.** Corporations must be incorporated with the Division of Corporations and pay a filing fee of around US $70. There are two types of corporation. A 'C' corporation pays its own taxes and is responsible for its own liabilities. The rate of corporation tax is 5.5 per cent. With an 'S' corporation up to 75 shareholders share the income and costs of the business and declare their shares on their individual tax returns.

Further information is available on the website for the Internal Revenue Service: www.irs.gov. There are helpful explanatory leaflets that can be downloaded: go to www.irs.gov/pub/irs for those relating to partnerships (Publication 541) and corporations (Publication 542), and to www.irs.gov/taxtopi for sole proprietorships (Tax Topic 408). It is also worthwhile taking a look at the website of the Division of Corporations for Florida: www.sunbiz.org.

State aid and other financial assistance

There are relatively few grants and subsidies to assist in starting a business in the United States, at least compared with the situation in most European countries. One publication, however,

The Complete Guide to Government Grants (not connected to the author or publisher of this book, despite its title: available from www.government-grants.org at a cost of US $30) claims that you are certain to obtain substantial financial grants if you follow its advice. In addition to grants to small businesses it covers home improvement, home buying, homeownership, health, education and training. There are also a variety of loan schemes that can be obtained from the US Small Business Administration, and a number designed for the high-tech sector, or businesses engaged in the defence industry. Details of federal grants can be found at www.cfda.gov and also at www.government-grants.com.

Business plans

You can obtain guidance in relation to business plans from the US Small Business Administration at www.sba.gov/starting_business/index.html. Assistance is also available from the University of North Florida Small Business Development Center (see www.sbdc.unif.edu), which provides a sample business plan and interactive programmes for writing professional business plans that you can access for a modest fee (go to 'Startingbusinessplans' on the above site).

Complying with regulations

You must ensure that you comply with the various regulations governing your business. There are federal (ie national) and state or county-level requirements. At federal level, you should file form SS-4 with the IRS. The IRS will then allocate a Federal Employer Identification Number (EIN). This form can be downloaded from the IRS website: www.irs.gov. Go to publications and search for IRS form SS-4. Alternatively telephone the IRS on +10 (800) 829 4933. You will thereafter have to file quarterly federal tax returns, and an annual unemployment tax return if you are an employer.

At a state level:

▌ All businesses trading under a name that is not the name of the proprietor must register the trading name with the Department of State. Corporations and limited partnerships are not required to do this if they are trading in their legal name, although otherwise they must. Registration does not protect the name, it is only to ensure that there is a public record of it, to enable government agencies and the public to trace businesses.

▌ You will probably need a state business or professional licence, and should make enquires about this. In Florida you can do this at the Florida Department of Business and Professional Regulations (www.myfloridalicense.com).

▌ You are required to collect and account for sales tax (as you would VAT in the United Kingdom), and

▌ You may also need to file a 'New Hire Reporting Form' for each new employee (in Florida see www.fl-newhire.com). The authorities require this information in their efforts to find parents who are failing to pay child support.

You will need to find out what additional obligations are required of you at a county or city level, such as building and planning regulations, licences and fees for the use of certain types of premises. You should contact the offices of the city clerk, the city building inspector and the county tax collector, as well as the county planning department (see Blue Pages of the local telephone directory). You should visit the local small business development centre, where you should find the contact details you require and information generally on the requirements of the local government bodies. In Florida a particularly useful site is www.floridasbdc.com, and so is www.stateofflorida.com for details of regulations and licensing requirements governing a wide range of business activities.

Employing others

In the United States an employer has to comply with not only national or federal regulations governing such matters as health and safety, family and medical leave, and labour standards and equal opportunity laws, but also various state provisions. The picture is complex, and you should give serious consideration to seeking advice from a labour lawyer.

Employers can obtain guidance on their obligations in respect of health and safety from the US Department of Labor Occupational Safety and Health Administration (see www.osha.gov/dcsp/ smallbusiness). The Fair Labor Standards Act provides that all businesses engaged in interstate business must pay a minimum wage, and that any time worked in excess of a 40-hour week must be paid at 50 per cent more than the usual hourly rate. There are strict controls on the employment of those under 16, and a prohibition on employing anyone under 18 for a range of dangerous employments. These rules apply to most employees, though there are exemptions for certain categories of employment, including white collar and computer professionals. The Family and Medical Care Act requires public sector employers and businesses employing more than 50 people to allow leave to employees in certain circumstances for up to 12 weeks per year. This covers parents following the birth, adoption or fostering of a child, and those who need to care for a spouse, child or parent. The leave is unpaid, but the employee's job is protected, as is his or her entitlement to health benefits.

Responsibility for the above measures rests with the United States Department of Labor (www.dol.gov, tel: +10 (866) 487 2365). In addition employers must conform to a host of regulations prohibiting discrimination on the grounds of sex, race, colour, religion, national origin and disability (see the website of the Equal Employment Opportunity Commission, www.eeoc.gov and also the website www.ada.gov). Florida law requires that all businesses with four or more employees must have insurance cover for workers' compensation, save that in the agricultural sector this only applies where there are five or more employees, and in the construction industry it applies to businesses with any employees.

Most other states have similar rules. There are additional restrictions in relation to the employment of children.

In Florida a workforce network has been created in an effort to assist small businesses taking on new employees, Employ Florida (see www.employflorida.net, and also www.WorkforceFlorida.com). It provides help in recruitment, vetting and referrals, assessing candidates' skills, and training for candidates and existing employees. The Incumbent Worker Program (IWP) arranges individualized training for employees throughout Florida.

Insurance

It is mandatory for businesses to have insurance cover for their vehicles, health insurance for their employees and property insurance. The notification period for claims is very short. You should keep your policy document in a safe place which you will be able to access in the event of an emergency. You should consider carefully with the insurers the extent and level of cover that you require.

Obviously all businesses require buildings insurance and public liability insurance. In several states, including Florida and California, you will also need to arrange cover for natural disasters, such as for flood and windstorm damage in Florida. You can obtain reasonable buildings and contents insurance against flood damage from the US government's National Flood Insurance Program (www.fema.gov/nfip). In some coastal areas, especially in the south-east and west central regions of Florida, you may find difficulty obtaining cover for windstorm damage. Wind-only policies are, however, available from the Citizens Property Insurance Corporation (www.citizensfla.com). Other risks that you should consider covering are business interruption to cover additional losses following flood or wind damage, insurance to cover your personal position as a director or company officer, and insurance to cover any losses to the business following the ill-health or death of a key employee. In Florida the Department of Financial Services produces a *Small-Business Owner's Insurance Consumer's Guide* (see its site at www.fldfs.com).

Useful contacts

British American Business Inc: www.babinc.org/links/jobsearch.html
United States Small Business Administration: www.sba.gov
US Department of Labor: www.dol.gov, tel: +10 (800) 972 7332
Department of Labor Occupational Safety and Health
Administration: www.osha.gov
Florida Small Business Development Centers:
www.floridasbdc.com
Florida Bar Lawyer Referral Service: www.flabar.org,
tel: +10 (800) 342 8011
Central California Small Business Development Centre:
www.ccsbdc.org
California Lawyer Referral Service:
www.california-lawyer-referral.org
Resource Guide: www.800helpfla.com. This site provides a
detailed A–Z resource guide to enable you to identify the agency
that you need to contact and to obtain the relevant contact details.
See also www.myflorida.com, www.ca.gov, www.oneflorida.org,
www.sunbiz.org, www.myfloridalicense.com,
www.americanbusinesslink.com, www.floridasmallbusiness.com
and www.sba.gov/starting_business

Publications

How to Start a Business in the USA, available from www.
immigrationagency.com (cost approx US $60).

Taking US nationality

A person who is a lawful permanent resident is permitted to live
and work in the United States indefinitely, and to sponsor certain
family members for immigration. He or she must also pay US
taxes. However, he or she is not a US citizen and cannot vote.

Those lawful permanent residents who have been *continuously*
resident in the United States for at least five years after gaining

the status of permanent resident are entitled to apply for naturalization. This can be reduced to three years for a person who has been married to and living with a US citizen for at least three years. There are a number of requirements, and applicants must check the up-to-date position. They include being of 'good moral character' (primarily not having a criminal conviction, or having been involved in criminal activity), swearing an oath of allegiance, undergoing an English language test, and also a civics test to assess the applicant's knowledge of US history and government. Applicants must also attend a naturalization interview. While the oath of allegiance involves renouncing all 'allegiance and fidelity' to any foreign state, the United States does permit its citizens and applicants for citizenship to have dual (or indeed multi-) nationality.

Before applying to become a US citizen (or indeed a citizen of any country), you should ensure that you are aware of both the advantages and the disadvantages. Your country of origin will not be prepared to interfere with any demands made upon you by your adopted country, such as military service. According to the Home Office, Her Majesty has no objection to British subjects applying for citizenship of a foreign state or states without losing their British nationality. The Canadian and Irish governments take the same permissive stance.

Further information

Liebman, Henry G (2004) *Getting into America: The immigration guide to finding a new life in the USA*, How to Books, Oxford
Shpigler, Debra R (2004) *How to Become a US Citizen*, Petersons, Lawrenceville, NJ
Jones, Roger (2005) *How to Get a Job in America*, How to Books, Oxford
Bureau of Citizenship and Immigration Services (BCIS) website: www.immigration.gov/graphics/howdoi/legpermres

9 Australia and New Zealand

Australia

Australia is the sixth largest country in the world, occupying an area as large as the US mainland, and almost twice the size of the European Union. While its population has increased fivefold over the last hundred years, it remains the country with the lowest population density in the world. Most Australians live along its stunning coastline, never far from one of the country's 7,000 beaches, or in one of the State and Territory capital cities.

The first reports of Europeans discovering Australia date from as early as the beginning of the 17th century, though it was not until towards the end of that century that a British explorer, William Dampier, landed on Australia's coast. It was another hundred years before Captain Cook claimed this huge continent for the British Crown. Over the following hundred years Australia served as a penal colony for some 150,000 convicts, the first of whom arrived on 26 January 1788, the day now celebrated as Australia Day. It was only in the late 18th century that the prisoners were followed by free immigrants, with the majority arriving from England, Scotland and Ireland. The Commonwealth of Australia was formed in 1901. One year later women received the right to vote, well over a decade earlier than in Britain. By that time the non-Aboriginal population of Australia amounted to no more than 3.8 million. The First World War, however, was to have a devastating impact on the nation. Of the 400,000 men who volunteered to fight in the distant war, 60,000 failed to return and many more were injured.

In the years since the end of the Second World War Australia has seen rapid expansion of both its economy and its population, with substantial further immigration not only from the British Isles but also from other parts of Europe, and in the more recent past from a much wider range of countries. Today the population of Australia stands at just over 20 million. While English remains the official language, Australia is extremely culturally diverse, with more than 4 million Australians speaking a second language.

The business and resident visa

This is for a period of four years, and is designed to enable those who have a skill in short supply to stay for a prolonged period in Australia. For some time now there have been shortages of skilled personnel in the legal and financial sectors, especially commercial lawyers, and a number of UK employment agencies regularly seek applicants on behalf of their Australian counterparts or Australian clients. Nurses, and in some areas teachers, are also in short supply. Those with vocational qualifications for a particular trade, such as joiners, electricians and plumbers, generally have no problem finding work, though they should arm themselves with their qualification certificates, and purchase the tools of their trade on arrival if they have not brought them with them. Those wishing to obtain a resident's visa in order to settle permanently definitely need a valued skill, and/or a family connection with Australia.

The working holiday visa

This visa is open to citizens of various countries including the United Kingdom, Ireland and Canada. Applicants must be aged between 18 and 30 and without children. It entitles holders to remain in Australia for up to 12 months, though they may not work for any one employer for more than four months. It is not possible to extend the duration of the visa, nor is it possible to obtain a second working holiday visa. Applicants must show that they have sufficient funds to purchase a return flight. Applications in the United Kingdom are processed by Australia House, Strand,

London WC2B 4LA (tel: +44 (0) 207 379 4334). Further details are available at www.immi.gov.au, where you can also apply online. Online applicants do not need to provide proof of having sufficient funds, nor do they have to provide their passport. A confirmation is generally provided within two days. This is sufficient to enable you to enter Australia on presentation of a valid UK passport. Should you overstay, it could jeopardize your prospects of obtaining a visa in the future. US citizens are limited to working for up to four months (on a Visa 416), but can remain a further three months on a tourist basis.

There are many agencies that will assist you in arranging a working holiday, including flights, guidance on finding your way around when you arrive, and advice on finding employment. Agencies often charge a hefty fee. You need to be certain what is included in the package before signing up to it. Organizations include BUNAC (www.bunac.org), IST Plus Ltd (www.istplus.com), Overseas Working Holidays (www.overseasworkingholidays.co.uk), Gap Activity Projects (GAP) Ltd (www.gap.org.uk), Travellers Contact Point (www.travellers.com.au) and Worldwide Workers (www.worldwideworkers.com).

There are many opportunities for those seeking temporary work in Australia, especially labouring, fruit picking (apples in Tasmania and Western Australia, grape picking in New South Wales, Victoria, South Australia and Western Australia, and banana picking in Queensland) and tourism (Queensland and the Gold Coast near Brisbane).

Working illegally

While this was quite commonplace in the past, employers now face substantial fines if they are caught employing anyone without a work visa, and accordingly they are reluctant to take on anyone who does not have the correct paperwork. Indeed the authorities exhort employers to report those working in breach of the rules. Labour shortages in the fruit-picking season can be so severe, however, that employers will take on workers who only have a tourist visa, despite the risks of a raid by officials of the

Department of Immigration and Multicultural and Indigenous Affairs (DIMIA).

Finding a job

I recommend that prior to leaving the United Kingdom you obtain the *Australia & New Zealand Independent Travellers' Guide,* available free online from www.tntmagazine.com.au. Take a look at the classified section on the TNT website (www.tntclassifieds.com.au), where you will also find the company's contact details.

The five main cities in Australia are Sydney, Melbourne, Perth, Adelaide and Brisbane. Sydney has the greatest number of opportunities partly owing to its size, but also because of its industrial sectors. It also has a higher cost of living than the other cities mentioned. The *Melbourne Age,* the *Courier and Mail* in Brisbane and the *Sydney Morning Herald* (www.smh.com.au) all have numerous job offers in their classified sections. Find out what time of day the papers you wish to consult are available, to ensure that you have an edge over the competition. While there are many employment opportunities in Australia, there is keen competition, including that from the many other foreigners legally and illegally searching for work. The two specialist books *Getting a Job in Australia* by Nick Vandome (2004) and *Living and Working in Australia* by Laura Veltman (2005) are both worth consulting, as are the government websites www.workplace.gov.au and www.jobsearch.gov.au. The services provided at the government's various job centres are only available to the long-term unemployed.

There are numerous Australian and international websites offering jobs in Australia, advice and assistance. These include www.jobmap.com.au and www.mycareer.com.au. There are of course numerous private employment agencies including Adecco, advertising positions across a range of industries including in particular secretarial and office work, administration, computing, financial services, the hotel trade and catering. Those arriving in Sydney in search of work should visit George Street where a number of the major agencies are located. Save in areas where there is an extremely high seasonal demand, such as the fruit-picking areas during harvest, or tourist resorts in high season, Australia employers generally demand references. Some posts require specialist qualifications, though these can often be satisfied by attending a short course lasting perhaps only a day, such as the Responsible Service of Alcohol Certificate for working in the hospitality industry.

Numerous jobs are available in the remoter parts of Australia on large farms and cattle stations, including in the provision of ancillary services such as catering for the farm and station workers. Several businesses offer training as jackaroos (assistants working on the cattle stations). At harvest time in particular, farm owners liaise with those running the country's many hostels in an attempt to recruit workers. Working in these remote areas can be rather unpleasant owing to a combination of the stifling heat, intense boredom, unpleasant insects, spiders and snakes. Women who undergo this experience have reported finding the sexist attitudes and often over-physical approaches of male fellow workers some-times difficult to tolerate. Another extremely demanding industry in which there is frequently a labour shortage is prawn fishing, for example off the coast at Darwin. This is definitely not for the faint-hearted, and anyone attracted by the high earnings offered would do well to speak to someone who has undergone this expe-rience. The prawn fishing season lasts for several months.

In the fertile fruit-growing areas, such as the Hunter Valley of New South Wales, the tropical Queensland coast and the beautiful island of Tasmania, conditions are a little more bearable, though farmers expect those taken on to work long hours. Australia is such a vast country, with such a variety of different fruits and other crops, that it is possible to move around the continent obtaining a succession of different harvest employments. In the warmer areas to the north, however, there are tropical fruits growing for much of the year, and many professional fruit pickers spend a large part of the time based in those areas. Probably the most comprehensive sources of job advertisements are www.goharvest.com and www.jobsearch.gov.au/harvesttrail. In some cases farmers, who are often desperate to recruit people to pick their crops, offer accommodation. If they do not, they will usually permit those taken on to put up a tent on their land.

Large numbers of visitors to Australia obtain employment at its many tourist and seaside resorts, especially along the eastern coast, including the many islands along the Barrier Reef. Those with qualifications and experience as divers generally find no difficulty in obtaining employment. For the more adventurous there are even possibilities in the hospitality industry on the islands much further off the coast, including Christmas Island and the Cocos Islands. Australia boasts a number of ski resorts, and again those with qualifications and experience in teaching this sport are in high demand. There is also a substantial demand for chefs, and for unskilled labour to work in the ski resorts. Those keen on visiting the Northern Territory might wish to seek employment at Ayers Rock Resort Village, which caters for the tens of thousands of visitors that flock to see Uluru (previously known as Ayers Rock) each year. A substantial number of people are required to look after these visitors, and recruits are often provided with accommodation. For further information search under employment on the website www.voyages.com.au.

While Australia is an English-speaking country, there is still a demand for teachers of English as a foreign language, primarily in the language schools such as the Universal English College (www.uec.edu.au), which cater for the many Asian students who visit Australia to learn the English language. Similarly there is a substantial requirement for nannies, especially those with a driving licence. Agencies include the Australian Nanny and Au Pair Connection (www.australiannannies.info) and in the United Kingdom, Childcare International (www.childint.co.uk).

Australia is such an immense country that there is a substantial demand for drivers, especially long-distance lorry drivers. Obviously a special driving licence is required, but some foreigners working in Australia have found obtaining one to be worthwhile.

Voluntary work

Australia has a large selection of opportunities to work as volunteers. In the field of conservation the first port of call is Conservation

Volunteers Australia (www.conservationvolunteers.com.au). If you are interested in farming work there are hundreds of organic farms in Australia regularly seeking to recruit workers. Contact World Wide Opportunities on Organic Farms (see its website for Australia, www.wwoof.com.au).

Tax

If you do not obtain a tax number you will be taxed at a rate of 49 per cent, rather than the standard rate of 29 per cent for non-residents. Those working in Australia under a resident's visa pay tax at the resident's rate of 17 per cent and are entitled to claim various allowances not available to non-residents. You can obtain a tax number from your local tax office. Details can be found at www.ato.gov.au.

All taxpayers should ascertain their entitlement to cover under the Medicare scheme.

New Zealand

It is often said that New Zealand is more British than Britain. Certainly it is true that a large majority of its population have family roots in the countries of the British Isles, and you will still hear the United Kingdom referred to as 'the old country'. New Zealand remains a favourite destination for Britons who decide to emigrate. The Queen remains the country's head of state, and its parliamentary system shares a great deal with that of the United Kingdom. Its legal system has much in common with that of England and Wales. Indeed the courts of New Zealand, like those of Australia, frequently make reference to decisions of the English courts, as both countries' laws are based on English common law, in which judges play an important role in making decisions and setting precedents.

New Zealand consists of two large islands, the North Island and the South Island, which together occupy an area slightly larger than the United Kingdom, but with a population of only 4 million.

The largest city is Auckland in the north of the North Island, and the capital is Wellington at the southern end of the North Island.

As many maps of the world omit Antarctica and much of the southern hemisphere, New Zealand can appear deceptively far south. In fact, the North Island is as far south of the Equator as Spain is north of the Equator, with the South Island as far south as France is north of the Equator. The North Island enjoys a wonderfully warm climate, though the more mountainous South Island is much cooler.

Entry requirements

UK citizens are entitled to stay in New Zealand without a visa for up to six months (Canadians and US citizens for up to three months). Occasionally visitors are required to produce a return ticket and proof that they have sufficient funds to keep themselves for the period of their stay.

To obtain a temporary work visa you will need an offer of employment, and your prospective employer must have demonstrated to the New Zealand Immigration Service that it is not practicable to fill the vacancy from among the unemployed in New Zealand. On arrival in New Zealand you must apply for a work permit, which will entitle you to stay in the country for up to three years. In the horticultural sector labour shortages are such that many visitors to New Zealand are able to work illegally, though the government is taking steps to combat this.

New Zealand also operates a scheme entitled the UK Citizens' Working Holiday Scheme, aimed at alleviating the country's labour shortages. This enables an unlimited number of UK citizens between the ages of 18 and 30 to obtain a working holiday visa (for further information see below). New Zealand has reached similar agreements with other countries, including Ireland and Canada. Those living in New Zealand under such visas may apply to extend their stay, and are entitled to apply for residence without having first to leave New Zealand.

Those who wish to emigrate permanently to New Zealand will find further information on the government's website (see above).

There are also various private advisory services that provide assistance, such as www.consylpublishing.co.uk. For further information see the extremely useful website www.immigration.govt.nz. This contains a detailed section on 'Settling in', with information about what to do prior to departure, on arrival, your rights, information centres, other free help and advice, transport, city maps and guides, accommodation, banking, telephones, emergencies and buying a car. The site also includes links to details of short-term and long-term job shortages.

Employment opportunities

New Zealand has a strong economy with labour shortages in many sectors, and is keen to attract people with skills and experience. While it is becoming a multiracial society, with many immigrants from Asia, it remains enthusiastic about immigration from the United Kingdom and Ireland, and other Anglo-Saxon countries whose citizens share a common heritage. For further information on job opportunities see www.dol.govt.nz, the website of the Department of Labour, and the classified sections of the *New Zealand Herald* (www.nzherald.co.nz).

A considerable number of British women who obtain work in New Zealand do so as administrators and secretaries in Auckland and Wellington, where there is a continual demand for those with experience. Another popular employment field for both men and women is telemarketing. Most opportunities are in the agricultural sector, tourism, the construction industry and in recent years also teaching. In most cases you will find that a car is essential.

New Zealand grows such a wide range of fruit and vegetables that there is almost a year-round demand for labour in its fields and orchards. Remuneration is modest, but on the other hand farmers can generally offer basic accommodation, and supply many of their own food products free of charge to their labourers. It is generally very easy to find agricultural labouring work by making enquiries in local shops and of farmers. Jobs are also advertised in the *New Zealand Herald*.

There are opportunities throughout the North and South Islands in catering and tourism, with particular demand for labour in Auckland, Queenstown and the ski resorts from around July to October. For those in the building trade there are currently opportunities in New Zealand's thriving construction industry (see for example the website of Allied Workforce, www.labourhire.co.nz, which claims to place 2,500 people daily).

New Zealand has a shortage of teachers, most notably at primary level, and has recruited a considerable number from the United Kingdom. Successful applicants may be entitled to a relocation grant. For further information see www.teachnz.govt.nz.

There are various organizations that organize work experience programmes in New Zealand, such as International Exchange Programs in New Zealand (www.iep.co.nz), the Work Experience Downunder programme (www.ccusaweusa.co.uk) and BUNAC. Agencies that will assist you in your search for employment include New Zealand Job Search (www.nzjs.co.nz), Kelly Services (www.kellyservices.co.uk), Adecco www.adecco.co.nz), Kiwi Recruitment (www.kiwirecruitment.co.nz) and Seasonal Work New Zealand (www.seasonalwork.co.nz). It is also worth taking a look at www.workingin-newzealand.com. The main newspapers to consult are the *New Zealand Herald* and the *Dominion Post* (in Wellington).

Applications for working holiday schemes

Britons can now apply online for these, as can the citizens of a number of other countries, including Canada, Ireland and the United States. There is a fee which must be paid by credit card. Postal applications are also acceptable, for which the same fee is payable. Your visa or permit is issued electronically, making the process quick and smooth. There is no need to part with your passport. Instead you will be asked to print out your visa or permit, which you must then keep with your passport. It is imperative that in completing your application you record the details correctly. These details will be consulted to determine your eligibility for a permit when you come to enter New

Zealand, and indeed your entitlement to enter a flight bound for New Zealand. It is possible to start filling out the online application form, save it and return to complete it at a later date. However, it should be noted that places under the scheme can fill up, so take care not to leave too long before you submit your application. Once you have submitted it, you should receive a message to confirm receipt. You can then consult the website to check on its progress. You should hear within a few days as to whether your application has been granted, or whether further information is required. There is no annual limit on how many UK citizens can be admitted under this scheme.

You will be issued with a number of entry visas when you receive your electronic visa or permit. This enables you to enter and leave New Zealand at will during the validity period of your work permit, though time spent outside of New Zealand cannot be added to the length of your work permit.

Applicants must be aged from 18 to 30 and are not permitted to take children with them. They must have a British passport with at least three months to run from the date of their intended departure from New Zealand, and be of good character (that is, they must not have certain criminal convictions or be a threat to the security of New Zealand). In addition they must be in possession of a return ticket, or sufficient funds to pay for a return ticket, and also funds of at least NV $350 for each month of their intended stay in New Zealand. UK citizens can opt for a 12-month or a 23-month visa. If you choose to apply for a 23-month visa you will need to undergo a medical examination and provide an X-ray certificate. If you obtain a 12-month visa and later wish to extend this, you may do so but will need at that point to undergo a medical and provide an X-ray certificate.

Those granted the visa must not accept permanent employment (unless they have also been granted an ordinary work permit). They are permitted to work up to a maximum period of 12 months.

Taxation

You must obtain a tax number from the Inland Revenue Department, or your earnings will be taxed at 46 per cent, over twice the level generally paid by non-residents. Details of its offices and other information can be obtained from the Department's website at www.ird.govt.nz. The Department does not generally investigate an applicant's immigration status, and even those working illegally in New Zealand have been able to reclaim some of the excess tax they have overpaid.

10 Turkey, Israel and the Middle East

Turkey

Turkey is now engaged in discussions with the European Union with a view to membership, but it is worth remembering that its accession is likely to be some way off, and that in large part this is because of the country's record on human rights. There was substantial hostility towards the United States, the United Kingdom and to a lesser degree other English-speaking nations even before the Iraq war, and this has been significantly exacerbated by the conflict.

There are very few opportunities for westerners to work in Turkey, other than for the larger international companies with a presence in the country, and such employers generally transfer existing personnel or recruit Turkish citizens. Good starting points for those in search of employment are the Turko-British Association (www.tba.org.tr) and the Turkish-American Association (www.taa-ankara.org.tr).

Despite some hostility to the Anglo-Saxon nations, there is nevertheless a growing interest in learning English, caused by an awareness of the importance of the language in the modern world. A large number of educational establishments, especially in the private sector, have for some time regularly recruited native English speakers. By far the greatest concentration is in Istanbul. Even though not the country's capital, Istanbul remains its most important commercial centre. Language schools include Best English (www.bestenglish.com.tr) and English Centre (www.englishcentre.com). Remuneration is often significantly higher than in many other parts of the world. As a consequence of their desire to acquire English, many middle-class and wealthy Turkish families are keen to employ English-speaking nannies (see for example www.anglonannies.com).

Turkey is becoming an increasingly popular tourist destination, especially along its Aegean coast. In recent years a substantial number of westerners have been able to obtain employment in Istanbul and the main coastal resorts in travel agencies, shops, hotels, bars and restaurants.

There is a growing expatriate community of Britons who have chosen to retire to the Turkish coast, some of them running businesses. Those in search of work should make themselves known within the expatriate community as it is frequently a route to employment.

Most westerners working in Turkey, other than those transferred there by international employers, remain in the country on three-month tourist visas. This obliges them to leave the country before their visa expires, but it can be renewed on their return. Those who are more established apply for a work permit (for which a contract of employment is a huge advantage) or a residence permit. For further information see the Turkish embassy website in your home country (www.turkey.embassyhomepage.com).

Israel

Thirty years ago Israel was an extremely popular destination for young westerners keen to spend some months working abroad, with many choosing a short, or in many cases a long, stay on a *kibbutz*. The situation is now rather different. In part this is because of the escalating violence in recent years, but it is also because over a prolonged period the Israeli government has severely restricted the number of visas and work permits it grants, and has seriously cracked down on those working illegally. Employers run the risk of substantial fines for breaking the rules.

Apart from working on a *kibbutz* or a *moshav* (see below) or as a volunteer, there are hardly any work opportunities in Israel, though it is possible to obtain secretarial work. Even schools teaching English as a foreign language tend to recruit locally. In the past tourism was a major employer, but the political situation has caused a massive reduction in the demand for staff in catering and the hotel industry. There remain some opportunities, however, primarily in Tel Aviv and the most popular resorts, such as Eilat and Herzliya. The holiday season in Israeli begins at the end of October and runs through to March.

The *Jerusalem Post* (in English: www.jpost.com) generally carries a small selection of jobs that might be suitable for English speakers.

If you wish to work on a *kibbutz* or to engage in volunteer work, you will need a B4 volunteer visa. You can obtain this either prior to your entry into Israel (if you have a position already arranged) or while you are in Israel, for example under a tourist visa. It is valid for only three months, and can be renewed only once. It is subject to various restrictions, and will cease to be valid if you leave Israel, even if it has not expired by the time you return. It is obviously preferable to have a placement with a *kibbutz*, or other employment, arranged before you arrive. The immigration authorities can often appear rather unfriendly, and may well ask you to prove that you have sufficient funds to maintain yourself. If you have a written offer of a position, you should produce this to the immigration authorities. They will often let you apply for the B4 visa there and then.

Working on a *kibbutz*

A *kibbutz* is a type of working community in which the means of production are owned by the permanent participants. Thirty years ago working on *kibbutzim* was extremely popular with young westerners, with every year a fresh supply of several tens of thousands spending several weeks or months carrying out work – usually farm work – in return for board and lodging, the basic necessities and a modest US $100 a month. The work is hard, and often volunteers are regularly required to work well over 40 hours per week.

On the other hand, volunteers usually report that there is a very active social life around the *kibbutz*. The number of foreigners choosing this path has declined dramatically.

While traditionally *kibbutzim* were found in agriculture, a considerable number are engaged in manufacturing or the tourist industry. Applicants for a placement on a *kibbutz* must be at least 18, and generally under 40 (some *kibbutzim* have an older age limit), be fit and be able to stay for at least eight weeks. For further information about *kibbutzim* see www.kibbutzvolunteer.com and www.ketura.org.il. You can also contact the Kibbutz Representatives in the UK (tel: +44 (0)20 8458 9235, e-mail: enquiries@kibbutz.org.uk). For the United States information can be obtained at www.kibbutzprogramcenter.org, and for Australia at www.kibbutz.com.au.

Once in Israel volunteers can apply locally. The starting point is the Kibbutz Program Center, Volunteer Department, 18 Frishman St, Tel Aviv (for further details see www.kibbutz.org.il). You will need a medical certificate and proof of insurance cover, and a return ticket out of Israel.

A *moshav* is similar to a *kibbutz*. The essential difference is that participants own their own homes and machinery, but join together to sell and market their production. On a *moshav* 'volunteers' are paid a modest wage, but generally are thought to be required to work harder than on a *kibbutz*, with some reporting that they were expected to work more than 70 hours a week, with very little in the way of social life. *Moshavim* can vary, and some volunteers have had much better experiences. The numbers of *moshavim* have steadily increased over the last two or three decades, and they are now an extremely important feature of life in rural Israel.

Volunteer work

A volunteer programme that sends British adults between the ages of 18 and 25 to teach English in Israel operates under the umbrella of the British Council in London (see connectyouth. enquiries@britishcouncil.org). An organization called Unipal arranges for students to teach English to Palestinians in Lebanon (see www.unipal.org.uk). Information on other opportunities for volunteers can be obtained from the Christian Information Centre in Jerusalem (www.cicts.org). The Israeli Ministry of Foreign Affairs keeps details of opportunities for volunteer work on archaeological projects (see www.mfa.gov.il).

The Middle East

There are regular employment opportunities for those with specialist skills to obtain work in the oil-rich states of the Middle East. There is a wide range of possibilities for those with qualifications and/or experience, including positions in medicine, nursing, teaching, the construction industry and of course the oil industry. Salaries are attractive, and the cost of living is relatively low. Those seeking positions as teachers of English as a foreign language will generally need to be quite highly qualified and experienced in this field.

Visa requirements vary between the different states, as does the extent to which Islamic teachings impose restrictions on the daily lives of expatriates. Bahrain and Oman have to date been more tolerant of western lifestyles. Those who have obtained a position in the Middle East, or who are considering or seeking employment there, should consult the UK Embassy's website for their proposed host country.

11 The Third and Developing World

Africa

Africa is by far the world's poorest continent. Employment opportunities for westerners in Africa, as in most parts of the developing world, are extremely limited. The continent has a plentiful supply of cheap unskilled labour, often people living in extreme poverty. Furthermore many African states have difficult bureaucratic hurdles that foreigners have to overcome in order to live and to work in the country.

Large parts of western Africa, and much of northern Africa, are French-speaking. In most of the rest of the continent English is either an official language or is very widely spoken. In these countries most children are taught in English, and there is little call for teachers of English as a foreign language, although there are more opportunities in Egypt (primarily in Cairo) and Morocco (mostly in Casablanca). English teachers for schools are recruited from among the local population. There are opportunities to teach English and Mathematics in schools in Ghana and Kenya (see www.kenyahighcommission.com for information on work permits in Kenya).

Most westerners working in Africa are volunteers, primarily working for charitable organizations including Voluntary Service Overseas (www.vso.org.uk) and Médecins Sans Frontières, or government organizations such as the British Council and the US Peace Corps. Volunteers are frequently students carrying out a year's voluntary work abroad before starting university. In most cases living conditions are basic, and volunteers are often at risk of falling ill with disease, or in danger of being attacked.

South Africa

As in the rest of Africa, there is a plentiful supply of unskilled labour. There are opportunities for foreigners with specialist skills in the IT industry and as engineers. Various papers carry job advertisements, including the *South African Sunday Times*, the *Cape Times* and the *Star* and *Citizen* in Johannesburg. Those with qualifications can apply for a B1–159, a work seeker's permit (see www.southafricahouse.com). You can enter South Africa with this permit, but can only stay for up to three months. One possibility is to apply to BUNAC's Work South Africa programme, which is available to students under 30, who are entitled to work under the auspices of the scheme for up to 12 months.

Latin America

The countries of South and Central America, including Mexico to the north, all have ample supplies of unskilled labour. Westerners with specialist skills, such as engineers and IT experts, and with fluent Spanish, can generally find employment. So too can experienced translators, especially those with experience in translating technical, scientific or legal documentation. The opportunities for other westerners are extremely limited, and are generally restricted to the teaching of English as a foreign language. Teachers of English are in particularly high demand in Mexico because of its proximity to the United States, and in Chile, now one of the most prosperous states in Latin America. In Chile it is worth trying Berlitz and the British English Centre, to name just two of the main language schools in Santiago. In Central America Costa Rica has the most successful economy, and here also you will find a strong demand for English teachers. In the more prosperous cities across the continent there are openings for secretaries who are bilingual in

Spanish and English, and in Brazil for Portuguese and English speakers, most notably in law firms.

One of the best starting points is the local English-language press to be found in nearly all the capital cities of the larger countries of Latin America, such as the *Mexico City News*. Job seekers often find employment by placing advertisements in these papers. Many of those who do find positions do so through the local expatriate network, and accordingly it is worth making contact with the various English-speaking associations in your host country. You should visit the offices or website of the local British Institute (a websearch under *Instituto Britanico* will lead you to most of those in Latin America). The British Institute employs a number of English speakers as teachers. You will need to be under 30 and have Spanish or Portuguese to A level. In addition the Institute's offices often have notice boards on which those wishing to teach or learn English can place advertisements. In most capital cities you will also find branches of the British and American Chambers of Commerce. Sometimes they have advertisements for job positions suitable for English speakers on their websites. At the very least they could help you identify some British or American companies that might be worth approaching.

It should be noted that many westerners have found difficulties in extracting their earnings from their employers. Accordingly you should endeavour to come to an agreement that you are paid weekly, rather than monthly in arrears.

If you are intending to stay for a prolonged period of time it is advisable to obtain a work visa. In most countries the bureaucratic procedures and delays can be quite disheartening. You will need notarized copies of your qualifications and other documentation required. The majority of those remaining in Latin America for only a short time work on tourist visas, and either apply for extensions of these visas, or more often cross over into another country and return to their host country for a further period as a tourist.

Useful websites include www.mexicanconsulate.org.uk (with a section advising visitors wishing to work during their stay in Mexico); www.workingabroad.com, www.volunteerlatinamerica. com, www.afsuk.org (for short-term community service work for volunteers), www.icye.co.uk (Inter-Cultural Youth Exchange), www.volunteergalapagos.org and www.challengesworldwide.com.

A large number of westerners who visit Latin America do so as volunteers carrying out a wide range of tasks, often working on conservation projects. In many cases volunteers are required to pay a fee. Those speaking Spanish (Portuguese for projects in Brazil) will generally have a wide range of options.

The Caribbean

The opportunities to work in the Caribbean are limited. Those with experience of working on yachts are best placed to find employment. There are also positions in the tourist and leisure industries. Prospects of employment generally are probably highest in the Cayman Islands (which are English speaking and a former British possession) and the Dominican Republic (which is Spanish-speaking). Haiti (where the slaves brought to the island became free men following their revolt as early as 1791) remains an extremely volatile location which should be treated with extreme caution.

One of the most useful websites for the Caribbean is www.jobinthesun.com. At the time of writing there were vacancies for secretaries, accountants, teachers, IT specialists, water sports instructors, store managers, receptionists, chefs and various positions in legal and financial services. The site has links to www.caribbeanjobs.com and www.recruitsoffshore.com

Asia

As in other areas of the developing world the opportunities for westerners are extremely limited, save for those with specialist skills. This does not apply, of course, to Japan, which is already highly developed and has much in common with western economies. Two other exceptions are Singapore and Hong Kong. As China becomes more open to the western world this is also producing increasing opportunities for employment.

There is a continually increasing demand for the teaching of English as a foreign language, with demand being at its highest in Japan (where English teachers are highly paid compared with other parts of the world) and Thailand, followed by China, Korea and Taiwan.

Japan

It is difficult to obtain a teaching appointment before going to Japan, where many positions are filled by personal recommendation. Exceptions are appointments made through the Japan Exchange and Teaching Programme, which is open to English-speaking graduates aged under 40. The annual application deadline is towards the end of November. For further information see www.jet-uk.org. One private organization that recruits teachers in the United Kingdom is the Nova Group, 126 Regent Street, London W1R 5FE (www.teachinjapan.com). Alternatively a good starting point is to contact English speakers already in Japan to ask for guidance and to use the English-language press (most notably the *Japan Times*). The website www.metropolis.co.jp is worth a visit. Once in Japan many westerners make their way to the Kimi Information Centre in the Oscar Building in Tokyo (see website www.kimiwillbe.com) where you can obtain information and leads concerning both jobs and accommodation.

If you wish to obtain a work visa you will need a Japanese sponsor. Those who have employment arranged prior to arriving in Japan should ask their employer to take care of this. It is also possible, however, to be sponsored by a private individual Japanese citizen. Another possibility, generally restricted to those aged 18–25, is to apply for a working holiday visa, under which you are permitted to work in Japan for up to 12 months. Those entering on a student visa are limited to 20 hours' paid work per week.

Often westerners enter Japan as visitors, find employment and then apply for work visas. A visitor is entitled to stay for three months, and it is generally possible to obtain one extension for a further three months, giving a maximum of six months.

Japanese Embassy websites (in the United Kingdom, www.uk.
emb-japan.go.jp) contain further information on the range of
visas available.

South Korea

South Korea has a substantial demand for teachers of English,
with most posts traditionally filled by Americans. The South
Korean government operates the English Program in Korea
(EPIK) to recruit English speakers to work in the state school
system. Application is made through the Korean Embassy in your
home country (in the UK the address is 60 Buckingham Gate,
London SW1E 6AJ). Further information is available on the organization's website: www.epik.knue.ac.kr. As elsewhere, it is
generally worth consulting local English-language newspapers,
such as the *Korean Times* and the *Korean Herald*.

Taiwan

The people of Taiwan are extremely enthusiastic about learning
English, and university graduates in any subject have good
prospects of finding employment. Starting points are the website
www.taiwan-teachers.com (run by a teacher placement agency)
and the English language newspapers *China News* and *China Post*.
There are a number of sizeable English language schools requiring
a regular supply of English speakers, including Todd's English
School (www.toddsenglishschool.com). Note that tourists
entering Taiwan are entitled to stay for only two weeks, and
accordingly job seekers should apply for a 60-day visa before they
leave their home country. (For further information see the website
of the Bureau of Consular Affairs in Taiwan: www.boca.gov.tw.)
Once you have obtained employment your employer should
apply for a working permit. This will enable you to apply for a
resident's visa from the Ministry of Foreign Affairs and obtain an
Alien Resident Certificate from the local police.

Thailand

Thailand again has few job opportunities for foreigners, though many westerners are successful in obtaining employment teaching English as a foreign language. While technically a work permit is required, most westerners simply cross over the border into Malaysia every three months, thereby automatically renewing their tourist visas. Potential starting points for finding employment are the *Bangkok Post* (www.bangkokpostjobs.com), ECC (www.eccthai.com), the American University Language Centre (www.auathailand.org) and the British Council.

China

China offers very few opportunities for paid employment. The teaching of English, however, is growing rapidly here. The best starting points for prospective candidates are the British Council (www.britishcouncil.org/languageassistants), Voluntary Service Overseas, the China TEFL Network (www.chinatefl.com) and the website www.teach-in-china.cn.

Hong Kong

It has become more difficult for Britons to enter Hong Kong since its return to China in 1997. British citizens must apply for a work visa and will generally need confirmation of a job appointment in order to obtain one. Work visas are normally only granted where the position cannot be filled by a local resident. No visa is required in order to visit Hong Kong and to stay for up to six months, but it is difficult for those entering as visitors to then successfully apply for a work visa. Further information is available on the website www.info.gov.hk.

Starting points for obtaining employment in Hong Kong are the English-language newspapers *The Standard* and the *South China Morning Post*. In brief there are very few opportunities save in IT, secretarial work and the teaching of English. In many cases employers require a knowledge of Cantonese. Those seeking to teach English should visit the website of the Hong Kong government's Education and Manpower Bureau at www.embgov.hk.

India

India has few opportunities for paid employment, save for those with particular specialist skills working for international corporations. Most westerners working in India do so as volunteers, often under the auspices of a programme run from their home country, such as Voluntary Services Overseas, WWOOF, and the smaller Indian Volunteers for Community Service (www.ivcs.org.uk). A difficulty for those wishing to work in India, whether as volunteers or in paid employment, is obtaining a visa. Tourist visas are limited to a total of six months, and you are not permitted to apply for another visa while you are in India under a tourist visa. You should consult the website of the Indian Embassy in your home country (in the United Kingdom, www.hcilondon.net).

Useful addresses

British Embassies

See the website www.fco.gov.uk where you will find links to British embassies abroad (click on 'Most popular sections' and scroll down).

Foreign Embassies in the United Kingdom

See the website www.fco.gov.uk where you will find links to foreign embassies in the United Kingdom (click on 'Most popular sections' and scroll down).

Embassies generally

See www.embassyworld.com

General information

British Council

The British Council website (www.britcoun.org/home) has links and contact details for British Council offices in 110 countries (go to Contact Us on the home page).

British Chambers of Commerce and Industry

If you visit www.chamberonline.co.uk you will find contact details including links to websites for British Chambers of Commerce in most European countries. (Go to bottom left of home page, click on 'Contact your local chamber'. Go to right-hand side of next page, click on 'Council of British Chambers of Commerce in Continental Europe'.) For contact details of other British Chambers of Commerce worldwide (but currently no website links) go through the same route, but click on 'British Chambers of Commerce Overseas'.

Foreign Chambers of Commerce, abroad and in the United Kingdom

You will find contact information on all of these at www.chamberonline.co.uk (Go to bottom left of home page, click on 'Contact your local chamber'. Go to right-hand side of next page.)

Churches

Contact details of most Anglican churches are available from British consulates. For Anglican churches see www.anglicansonline.org.uk

Expat websites

There is an extensive selection of websites listed on the Back in Blighty website www.backinblighty.com (see 'expat links').

Cultural information

French

L'Institut Français
Queensbury Place, London SW7 2DT. Tel: +44 (0)207 834 2144, website: www.francealacarte.org.uk. Arranges tuition (including

telephone classes) and has a multimedia library, newspapers, restaurant and language facilities. French films are regularly shown, and other cultural events are arranged. There are a number of French shops close by, a children's library (tel: +44 (0)207 838 2144) and the French Bookshop (tel: +44 (0)207 584 2840).

Centre Français de Londres
61 Chepstow Place, London W2 4TR. (tel 0207 7920337).

There are also French cultural centres in Bath, Bristol, Cambridge, Exeter, Glasgow, Jersey, Milton Keynes, Manchester, Oxford and York.

Alliance Française
The *Alliance Française* holds courses to teach French throughout France, in England and elsewhere. For details of courses in the United Kingdom tel: +44 (0)207 723 6439.

Spanish

Instituto Cervantes
102 Eaton Square, London SW1 9AN. Tel: +44 (0)207 235 0353, website: www.cervantes.es

Instituto Cervantes has many centres around the world providing information about Spain, Spanish culture and the Spanish language. To locate the centres across the world go to its website and click on '*IC en el mundo*' at the top of the home page.

Italian

The Italian Cultural Institute in London provides information about Italy, Italian culture, and the Italian language: 39 Belgrave Square, London SW1X 8NX, tel: +44 (0)207 235 1461; fax: +44 (0)207 235 4618, website: www.icilondon.esteri.it. You can find a good number of branches of Italian Cultural Institutes around the world by searching under *Instituto italiano di cultura*.

Portuguese

You can find links to several sites about Portuguese culture and language on the website of the Portuguese Centre: www.clpic.ox.ac.uk

World cultures

The website www.peoplegoingglobal.com has a wide range of information about different countries of the world.

Learning languages

www.europa-pages.co.uk has a directory of schools, colleges and universities offering foreign language tuition (Spanish and French).

Careers

Careers Research and Advisory Centre, Bateman Street, Cambridge CB2 1LZ. Tel: +44 (0)1223 460277, website: www.crac.org.uk
Intercultural Educational Programme, 33 Seymour Place, London W1H 5AP. Tel: 0+44(0)20 7402 3305.

Volunteering

Voluntary Service Overseas: www.vso.org.uk
International Voluntary Service: www.ivs-gb.org.uk

Removal firms

General websites

www.removers.org.uk
www.intlmovers.com

Commercial firms

Allied Pickfords: www.gb.allied.com
Britannia Bradshaw International:
www.bradshawinternational.com
Overs International: www.overs.co.uk, tel: +44 (0)1252 343646
Worldwide Shipping & Air: +44 (0)23 80633660
Freight Co: www.worldfreight.co.uk

Transport

Airlines

Aer Arran: www.aerarann.ie
Air Cyprus: www.cyprusairways.com
Air France: www.airfrance.co.uk, tel: +44 (0)845 0845 111
Air Malta: www.airmalta.com
Alitalia: www.alitalia.com
Britair: www.britair.fr, tel: +44 (0)8 20 820820
British Airways: www.britishairways.com
British European: www.flybe.com
BMI Baby: www.flybmi.com
easyJet: www.easyjet.co.uk
Globespan: www.globespan.com
Iberia: www.iberia.com
Jet 2: www.jet2.co.uk
Monarch: www.flymonarch.com
Qantas: www.qantas.com.au
Ryanair: www.ryanair.com
Thomsonfly: www.thomsonfly.com

Ferries

Brittany Ferries: www.brittany-ferries.com, tel: +44 (0)870 556 1600
Condor: www.condorferries.co.uk, tel: +44 (0)845 345 2000
Hoverspeed: www.hoverspeed.com, tel: +44 (0)870 524 0241
Irish Ferries: www.irishferries.ie, tel: +44 (0)870 517 1717
Norfolkline: www.norfolkline.com, tel: +44 (0)870 870 1020
P & O Ferries: www.posl.com, tel: +44 (0)870 600 0600
P & O Portsmouth: www.poportsmouth.com,
tel: +44 (0)870 242 4999
Sea France: www.seafrance.com, tel: +44 (0)870 571 1711
Transmanche: www.transmancheferries.com,
tel: +44 (0)800 9171201

Rail

www.raileurope.co.uk, tel: +44 (0)870 5848848
www.frenchmotorail.com, tel: +44 (0)870 2415415
www.eurotunnel.com, tel: +44 (0)870 5353535

Road and route planning

www.theaa.com
www.rac.co.uk
www.michelin-travel.com
www.mappy.com

References and further reading

There are a substantial number of books relating to living and working abroad, or in the individual countries listed in the text, including the following.

Spain

Davey, Charles (2004) *The Complete Guide to Buying Property in Spain*, Kogan Page, London

Davey, Charles (2005) *The Complete Guide to Living and Working in Spain*, Kogan Page, London

Ellingham, Mark and Fisher, John (2004) *The Rough Guide to Spain*, Rough Guides, London

Hampshire, David (2005) *Living and Working in Spain*, Survival Books, Fleet

Hobbs, Guy (2004) *Starting a Business in Spain*, Vacation Work Publications, Oxford

Searl, David, (2004) *You and the Law in Spain*, Santana Books, Spain

France

Biggins, Alan (2002) *Selling French Dreams*, Kirkdale Books

Brame, Genevieve (2004) *Chez vous en France*, Kogan Page, London

Davey, Charles (2005) *The Complete Guide to Buying Property in France*, Kogan Page, London

Davey, Charles (2006) *The Tee Guide to Living and Working in France*, Stanley Tee, Bishop's Stortford

Hampshire, David (2005) *Living and Working in France*, Survival Books, Fleet

Hart, Alan (2004) *Going to Live in Paris*, How to Books, Oxford

Hunt, Deborah (2003) *Starting and Running a B&B in France*, How to Books, Oxford

Platt, Polly (2003) *French or Foe?* Cultural Crossings

Italy

Carlisle, Kate (2005) *Living and Working in Italy*, Cadogan, London

Greece

Reynolds, Peter (2005) *Going to Live in Greece: Your practical guide to living and working in Greece*, How to Books, Oxford

Portugal

Barrow, Colin (2005) *The Complete Guide to Buying Property in Portugal: Buying, renting, letting, selling*, Kogan Page, London

Hobbs, Guy (2005) *Living and Work in Portugal*, Vacation Work Publications, Oxford

United States

Davey, Charles (2005) *The Complete Guide to Buying Property in Florida*, Kogan Page, London

Hampshire, David (2004) *Buying a Home in Florida*, Survival Books, Fleet

Jones, Roger (2005) *How to Get a Job in America*, How to Books, Oxford

Liebman, Henry G (2004) *Getting into America: The immigration guide to finding a new life in the USA*, How to Books, Oxford

Moen, Christian and Howell, John (2006) *Buying a Property in Florida*, Cadogan, London

Peterson's (2003) *Summer Jobs in the USA*, Petersons, Lawrenceville, NJ

Shpigler, Debra R (2004) *How to Become a US Citizen*, Peterson's, Lawrenceville, NJ

Australia and New Zealand

Collins, Matthew and Neilson, Mary (2004) *Going to Live in New Zealand*, How to Books, Oxford

Pallfy, Georgina (2005) *Working and Living in New Zealand,* Cadogan, London

TNT (2006) *Australia/New Zealand Independent Travel Guide* [online]www.tntmagazine.com.au (accessed 3 April 2006)

Vandome, Nick (2004) *Getting a Job in Australia,* How to Books, Oxford

Veltman, Laura (2005), *Living and Working in Australia*, How to Books, Oxford

General

Griffith, Susan (2004) *Teaching English Abroad*, Vacation Work Publications, Oxford

Griffith, Susan (2006) *The Au Pair and Nanny's Guide to Working Abroad,* Vacation Work Publications, Oxford

Vandome, Nick (2005) *Planning Your Gap Year*, How to Books, Oxford

Wilson, Mark (2004) The Medic's Guide to Work and Electives Around the World, Hodder Arnold, London

How to (2004) *Worldwide Volunteering*, How to Books, Oxford

Woodworth, David and Pybus, Victoria (2005) *Summer Jobs Abroad*, Vacation Work, Oxford

Index

Index of advertisers